GOOD
BEHAVIOR

GOOD BEHAVIOR

NATHAN L. HENRY

BLOOMSBURY

NEW YORK BERLIN LONDON

First published in the United States of America in July 2010
by Bloomsbury Books for Young Readers
www.bloomsburyteens.com

For information about permission to reproduce selections from this book, write to
Permissions, Bloomsbury BFYR, 175 Fifth Avenue, New York, New York 10010

Library of Congress Cataloging-in-Publication Data
Henry, Nathan L.
Good behavior / by Nathan L. Henry. — 1st U.S. ed.
p.   cm.
ISBN 978-1-59990-471-9
1. Henry, Nathan L.   2. Prisoners—United States—Biography.   3. Criminals—
United States—Biography.   4. Juvenile delinquents—United States—
Biography.   I. Title.
HV9468.H44 A3 2010   365'.42092—dc22   [B]   2009050684

Book design by Danielle Delaney
Typeset by Westchester Book Composition
Printed in the U.S.A. by Worldcolor Fairfield, Pennsylvania
2 4 6 8 10 9 7 5 3 1

I dedicate this book to my dad (the rough edges and the soft parts of him), a man whom I respect and love, a man without whom I might have turned out to be something truly awful, or at least a lot less interesting—I might have become average and well-balanced, and nobody wants that.

GOOD
BEHAVIOR

[ONE]

Limped in through Sallyport in handcuffs, clothes caked in dried mud—sat down, exhausted, answered a million pointless questions.

"How old are you?"

"Sixteen."

"Allergies?"

"No."

"Physical handicaps?"

"I've been attacked by a police dog. I have four holes in my thigh."

"Doesn't count."

"But they let him chew on me for ten minutes."

"Still doesn't count." The guard looked up from his paperwork. "You know what a handicap is, right?" I nodded my head. "So aside from the holes in your thigh, do you have any?"

"No."

"Okay."

He was a black guy, the guard who processed me. He seemed three feet taller than me. He said his name was Dennis. He took my mug shot, let me take a shower, and gave me an orange jumpsuit and flip-flops. I moved through it all in a daze. I did what I was told.

I'd thought Philip and I would be sent back to Indiana, to the juvenile detention center in Mercantile. Juvie wasn't bad—I'd been there before. We could've sat around with the other losers and talked about what badasses we were. They would have worshipped us.

But I was booked into a county jail in Illinois. A *real* jail, where they kept rapists and killers and cannibals locked up—a place where I was sure that guys like me, scrawny sixteen-year-old kids who thought they were hot shit on the outside, were regularly raped, killed, and eaten by real criminals.

After Dennis snapped my photo I asked him, "How long could I get for this, man?"

He said, "For armed robbery? Hmm . . ." He thought. "Fourteen years maybe."

"Oh, Jesus." I almost fainted.

He took me to a cell and held the door for me. I limped in and he shut it behind me, turned the keys, and locked it. I stopped in the center of the cell and looked around. Bunk, sink, toilet. Nothing else. I heard the guard walk away and I turned around, and there was the door, shut and locked. I knew it was locked, but I walked up to it and pushed on it anyway. The reality of it crushed me, the absolute fact of what had taken place and where I was now, the unalterable nature of it, the certainty of it just squeezed into me, and I sat down on my bunk and closed my eyes. I eventually lay down and fell asleep.

— — —

Evening. Just before dark. My cell door opened. A guard, not Dennis but somebody else, an older, rounder white guy, said, "Detective's gonna take you over to make a statement."

I stood up. "Okay."

The detective looked like he was straight out of a bad eighties crime drama. His tie even had a palm tree on it, and he had a powder blue sports coat on. He had a thick mustache and he wore bluesman sunglasses, and walked like he had the drop on the whole goddamn world. I shuffled behind him, barely able to keep up. He seemed to have forgotten that I was in shackles and handcuffs. And that my leg had been mauled by a German shepherd.

We walked for ten minutes, past the courthouse, which was much more impressive, more imposing than any I'd ever seen—there was more brass, and the granite seemed somehow thicker, heavier than it should have been—to an administration building. He opened the door for me, but when I slipped on the stairs and struggled to get back up, he looked away and waited.

We entered a room full of desks and chairs and people talking on phones and people shuffling papers around and cops that looked just like him with their feet on their desks picking their teeth with what I imagined to be human bones. Then I noticed, at a large conference table in the center of the room, seated, with his head down on one arm, his other arm dangling beside him, handcuffed to the chair, was Philip. He was asleep. The detective and I walked by Philip, and as we passed, I kicked his chair.

"Wake up, fucker." He looked up without seeming to recognize me. I smiled at him. Philip was fourteen years old, blond and slender, and looked like he'd spent the day having a confession tortured out of him. As it turned out, he was just exhausted.

We went into another room, a smaller room, but this one was full of comfortable chairs, like a waiting room in a hospital—and everyone was there: my mom, my dad, my brother, Philip's mom and dad. I was so surprised by this that all I could say was, "Mom, I got bit by a dog," as I limped toward her.

She stood and said, "I know." Then she hugged me. Everyone else remained seated and silent. They watched me. They were disappointed, but not exactly shocked.

The detective said, "Your parents have agreed to let you speak with me. So we're going to have a conversation about what happened last night."

I looked around. My brother stared at me, no expression on his face, and Dad nodded his head. Dad said, kind of deadpan, "Go ahead and tell him what happened, Nate. Philip already talked."

The detective took me by the arm and walked me down a hall and into a tiny interrogation room with one table, two chairs, and a tape recorder. The walls were soundproof and there was a two-way mirror on one wall. He gestured for me to sit, so I sat.

"Let's talk about last night," he said as he took a seat and flipped the tape recorder on. He leaned back, threw his hands behind his head, and settled in.

The statement took a long time to record—about an hour—and I told him almost everything that had happened that night. Why not? I was already fucked. When we left the interrogation chamber, my parents were gone. We walked back over to the jail, and I was once again locked in.

P-1: private cell number one down on the first floor of the Paradise County Jail. It was a bit larger than the other cells, because it was designed to house two inmates. The main difference was its size and the number of bunks. There were also two steel shelves, about eight by twelve inches, bolted to the wall five feet off the floor between the bunks and the toilet; in a single cell there was only one. Everything else was the same. Blue paint on the floor and up the walls to about four feet, and then white from there to the ceiling, which was also white. The paint was high gloss, and there was a fluorescent light on the wall, two long rods brighter than the sun, encased in unbreakable Plexiglas. There were no shadows. There was one small window, three feet high and four inches wide—unbreakable two-inch-thick riot glass.

I looked through this thin slit of a window and watched people pass on the sidewalk twenty feet away. I felt like a caged freak. I was shocked that people didn't actually approach the glass and look in at me, tap on the window to get my attention, hope that I'd do something disgusting to amuse them, like masturbate wildly or eat my own feces.

No one gathered outside my window. No one gawked. No one was curious. They all just walked on by, and I was invisible.

[TWO]

Trick or treat night. I was seven years old. We were driving home from begging for candy in another town, and I was in the front seat sitting between my parents, exhausted from trekking around all night, with a big bag of candy on my lap. Dad was screaming at Mom. I don't know what the argument was about. It probably wasn't even an argument, just my dad screaming. It seems like he did that a lot, fabricated conflict just to clear his lungs. At some point Mom lost her temper—astonishing because Mom never lost her temper—and she slammed on the brakes as hard as she could. I almost flew through the windshield, but Dad slammed his right palm against the dash and his other palm against my chest and held me back against the seat. My brother smashed into the back of our seat. I couldn't breathe. A wave of terror froze me as I watched my bag of candy explode. The candy went everywhere.

Dad yelled, "What the fuck is wrong with you? I'm not riding in this goddamn car." And he threw open his door and got out. "I'm fucking walking home."

Mom didn't drive immediately. We sat there for a minute and watched Dad walk away, on the shoulder of the road, half in the gravel and half on the pavement, illuminated by our headlights. Just an hour before, we'd been rushing from house to house, filling our bags with booty, and I'd been mad with excitement, intoxicated with it, and it seemed to me, even though it surely wasn't the case, that Mom and Dad had felt that too. And now this. Dad had a limp because one of his legs was half an inch shorter than the other, but now he limped like it was half a *foot* shorter. It was comical how pathetic he looked, pissed off, walking a country road alone in the middle of nowhere after dark. I was afraid that Mom was going to run him over. I'd seen this in so many movies— Dad let me watch the worst fucking movies: gangster movies, Hells Angels movies, vigilante movies, serial killer movies.

I said, "Mom, you gonna run him over?"

She squeezed my leg. "No, Natey, but I should."

Instead of killing him, she drove up slowly beside him.

"Get in, Hank," she said. "Let's go home."

He didn't even look in the car. He was defying us. "Fuck you!" he yelled, as if we were a hundred yards away, out in the middle of one of those soybean fields.

Mom slammed her foot down on the accelerator and we drove off.

After a few moments, I asked her, "You really gonna let him walk, Mom?"

"That's what he wants." And she shrugged a little.

— — —

Dad finally got home three or four hours later, completely exhausted, collapsed on the couch, and fell asleep. Dad always slept with his legs curled up and his hands together under his cheek like a little kid, like that stereotypical way angelic little kids are supposed to look when they sleep. It always astounded me. What a crazy son of a bitch—that's the way he sleeps? You'd think he'd doze lightly on his back with a .357 Magnum in his hand. Like that scene in *Bonnie and Clyde* where the cops all file into the bedroom after a big shoot-out, find a guy lying on a bed with a sheet over him. They've got about fifteen guns on him, and they slowly peel back the sheet. The guy's awake, fully clothed, with a tommy gun in each hand stretched out along each of his legs. That's how I imagined Dad should've slept.

— — —

My mom was the Buddha. She never killed a thing in her life. In all my greatest moods, those too-brief shining moments of serenity when I am cognizant of certain wisdoms that are normally beyond my reach, I am reminded of the kinds of things that my mom has always said.

When I was a racist teenager, I'd say things like, "I hate niggers, Mom. They're mud people. I hate gooks and spics and faggots and old people and babies and women, except for you, Mom. I love you. But the rest of them should burn!"

She'd lay a saintly smile on me and say, "Nate, you don't even know those people. They're just trying to live their lives and find happiness. You shouldn't hate so much—it's not good for you."

My dad, on the other hand, was practically a serial killer. "Nate," he'd say, "just imagine, you could have your pick. Just go out in a van and find one you like, take her home, and put her in your basement. Just think how great that would be." Or, "Women are all the same, Nate. Chop their heads off and they all look alike."

[THREE]

Early the next morning, I was taken to the courthouse for my arraignment. My parents were there. The place was packed with people, and I was disoriented. I was ushered up to a podium in front of the judge, who said to me, "Mr. Henry, you're being charged, as an adult, with armed robbery, a first-degree felony. Do you understand the charge?"

"Yes," I said. I didn't understand. I wasn't exactly clear on what an arraignment was, and I had just been jarred from deep sleep into a reality that completely stunned me.

"Do you wish to enter a plea?"

"I'm guilty, I guess."

The judge looked down at me. He sort of sighed and leaned forward. "I'm going to enter a not-guilty plea for you."

"Okay."

"The prosecutor and your attorney will work out a deal that way, but if you enter a plea of guilty right now, I'll have to sentence you, and I don't think you want that yet."

"No, sir. I don't."

"Okay, then we'll enter a not-guilty plea."

At the time I didn't realize how astonishingly lucky I was to have such a reasonable and considerate judge. Only years later would I see what an oddly singular action this was. How many judges pounce on ignorant, confused guilty pleas? It could have been the end of me right then.

After the arraignment, I stood outside of the courtroom with the guard who had taken me there. My parents stood close to me.

After the robbery that night, after the chase and everything, when I'd stood in the cornfield with the gun, considering whether or not to rush out and open fire on the cops, I remember all I really wanted to do was call Mom and tell her how sorry I was. You hear all those stories about soldiers and criminals yelling for their mothers as they die, which always sounded strange to me, but that's just what I wanted when I was facing possible death. I wanted my mom.

"Mom," I said, "I was talking to this guard who booked me yesterday, and he said I could get fourteen years."

She smiled a very painful smile and ran her hand through my hair. "Don't think about that, honey."

"You'll be all right, Nate," Dad said.

I couldn't speak. I wanted to cry.

"Come on, Henry," the guard said. "Time to go back."

Mom hugged me and I was led off back to the jail in my shackles and handcuffs, certain I was doomed.

— — —

For the first couple of weeks that I was in jail, I was in a strange form of shock. I wasn't allowed to smoke, so a good deal of this shock must have been due to nicotine withdrawal. Everyone I saw seemed familiar to me, as if I had met them before in a dream. Everyone—all the guards, all the inmates—seemed nostalgically connected to my past, an ancient past of which my current incarnation was unaware. I dreamed of smoking cigarettes, of Joan and Philip, and I awoke every day surprised to find myself still there in jail, still locked in a concrete cell.

I got a cellmate not long after I arrived. I remember the moment he bounced into my cell behind a grocery cart containing his mattress and a gray plastic tub full of his belongings. He did seem to bounce. He was an overwhelming presence, dark skin, olive, and a big blond Afro atop his head the diameter of a small automobile tire. He was much bigger than me, dressed in a white T-shirt and sweatpants, and he had muscular arms. The way he moved, the way his hair bobbed around, he was like a cartoon character.

Arnold, seventeen years old. I think he was in for burglary, but as with all my later cellmates, he told me stories, plenty of stories, of other crimes he wasn't caught for, some of them pretty fucking scary. Arnold's parents were Southern Baptist fanatics, and by the time I met him he had reembraced the faith of his youth.

So Arnold was all aflush with Jesus and the good news. He asked his parents to bring me a Bible, which they did, and which I read lazily. I hadn't caught on to the routine yet, so I wasn't aware that a library cart circulated once a week, pushed around the entire jail, from cell to cell, by a little librarian from the city library who could get you almost any book you asked for. She would later become very important to me.

For now, I discussed religion with Arnold. I told him I'd been a Satanist for a couple of years, but wasn't sure what any of it really meant.

He said, "*My* God will forgive you. What's your worst sin?"

I said, "I don't know."

"Did you ever blaspheme the Holy Spirit?"

"Sure," I said. "I blaspheme the Holy Spirit all the time."

This threw Arnold into severe doubt as to whether I was actually savable, but after much deliberation he finally decided that I was. I pretended to be relieved.

P-1 was on the first floor next to Sallyport, and right outside my cell door was the table where the guards would sign in new inmates. On weekends, there'd be a parade of drunks and degenerates, fighting with the cops, pissing down their legs, puking on the table. You might think the spectacle would be something worth looking forward to, but in reality it just meant noise—lots and lots

14

of noise. I watched the guards subdue belligerent drunks, would-be suicides bang their heads on my cell door with half a dozen guards on top of them, girls drunk and underage try to strip off their clothes—this was nice, but rare.

The crazies were the worst. P-1 was at the intersection of two hallways, with the suicide-watch cells straight ahead of my cell door so their doors were visible to me. There was one crazy who looked just like Charles Manson—somehow all crazies manage to look just like Manson—and was on suicide watch for weeks. During rec one day he managed to get hold of a tiny, thin strip of plastic. With this he dug through the skin on his arm and extracted a vein, which he then chewed through. I watched the guards gather outside his cell door with their rubber gloves on; then they opened his door and rushed him. When the door swung open, I saw blood smeared all over it. After moments of scuffle, they dragged him out and pinned him to the floor of the hallway. He was screaming, covered with blood. When the medics finally arrived, they strapped him to a gurney, and he looked right into my eyes as they wheeled him out through Sallyport. I've never seen such misery in a human being.

My parents came to visit me often. My mom came every week, either with Dad or with my brother. They would stand outside my cell and we'd speak through the little window in my cell door.

I told my mom on the phone that I was checking out the Bible, not because I was seriously *checking it out* but because I thought this might be something she'd like to hear.

She said, "Don't tell your dad or your brother about that."

So I didn't say anything else about it. This wasn't because they'd have much of an opinion about whether or not I believed in God, but because everyone knows how pathetic and exceptionally phony jailhouse religion looks.

[FOUR]

I grew up in a small town—a *very* small town. Brickville is about forty miles west of Indianapolis, out in the flat country, surrounded by infinite corn and soybean fields. There are just around four hundred houses in Brickville, and one stoplight. It takes less than ten minutes to walk from one edge of town to the other.

There was once a bar, but it closed up. There is no police department in town. If anything happened, you called the sheriff's department, and it took them forty-five minutes to get there. Public fights seemed relatively common.

Our house was a run-down hundred-year-old structure, fairly large but falling apart. On the side of the house, the external wall of our living room bulged out mysteriously. It was as if the house had a tumor. My dad eventually tore the wall out and replaced it. Dad was constantly working on the house. But he painted it all—all of it—battleship gray. It looked like a small prison.

I remember one day when I was eight my brother, Jim, and I were playing in the alley beside our house and this drunk stumbled down it, holding a hand to his head. He had blood all over his shirt, and before he spoke to us he spat out a mouthful of blood. This was before they paved the alley, so when the glob of spit hit the ground, it immediately soaked into the dirt. I couldn't take my eyes off the red spot of mud. The guy asked if we had a wet towel he could use to clean up before he went home to his wife, so my brother went into the house and got a bowl of warm water, a washcloth, and a towel.

We watched the guy wipe off his face. I didn't say a word the whole time. I just watched the pink water drip from the guy's chin, watched swirls of red go round and round in the bowl.

My brother, who is five years older than me, said, "So, what'd you do, get in a fight?"

The guy said, "Looks that way, doesn't it?"

After he was clean, he thanked us and walked on.

— — —

There was a mural on the side of a building right in the center of Brickville. At the top it said THE ROLL OF HONOR, and underneath were hundreds of names of people who died in foreign wars. The mural was red, white, and blue, with American flags all over it. Beneath the mural, jutting out into the sidewalk, was a stoop, where a group of hoods could generally be found hanging out, either on the stoop or around the corner in the pizza shop.

At any given time, there were really very few people on the streets of Brickville. It was a very slow, quiet little town. It was a farm community, but there were several factories nearby. The people who lived there were either farmers or factory workers. The houses were clean and the lawns were well kept, and the farmers gathered at the diner every morning right across the street from my house. Brickville was busiest first thing in the morning, and at around ten it went quiet again. At four p.m. the shifts at the factories ended, and the factory workers headed to the carryout next door to my house for a six-pack of beer and cigarettes; the school buses brought the kids back to town around the same time, so things got kind of festive then.

There was a feeling in Brickville of being entirely isolated. The rest of the world happened in some far-off exotic place. The names of great cities and other countries were mispronounced, because they felt so unnatural in the mouths of Brickville citizens. Anything that happened outside our county was something dubious and unnecessary.

It was a genuinely safe place to grow up, and nothing ever changed there.

Of course my dad couldn't appreciate this, and so neither could I. If I was standing near a window and the light cast my silhouette on the shades, Dad would say, "Get away from there. You never know what kind of sick fucker's out there. Remember the .22 killer. Shot people through their windows."

"What," I remember him asking my mom, "if there was a bunch of Manson Family members camping in the lot over here?"

"I hope they wouldn't be," Mom said.

"What if they were?"

"Who are the Mansons?" I asked.

"Never mind, Natey," Mom said.

"They come in at night and cut you up in your sleep," Dad told me. "It can happen. Believe me. They cut a baby out of a pregnant woman."

"They didn't catch them?" I ask.

"Not all of them. They could be anywhere."

And he was dead serious.

So I never felt that Brickville was safe. I never felt that anywhere was safe. The farmers who gathered at the diner across the street were the same kind of farmers who mobbed together with torches and lynched people they didn't like, and the factory workers were thieves and rapists and liars you couldn't trust, and the Manson Family could turn up at any time, anywhere.

— — —

I was probably nine years old. Dad was washing up in the bathroom one morning and I was sitting at the dining room table playing with a Matchbox car.

Dad said, "Nate, go get my shirt off the floor in the living room."

We didn't have air-conditioning, so during the

summer months Mom and Dad would drag their mattress downstairs and sleep on it in the living room. His shirt was beside the mattress. I grabbed his shirt and a revolver fell out of it onto the floor. I picked it up, looked around. What the hell?

I had the gun in one hand and his shirt in the other, standing in the doorway of the bathroom, when he looked over from his shaving.

Truly shocked, he said, "What are you doing with that?"

"It was in your shirt."

"How'd it get there?" He took it from me.

"I don't know."

He believed me, but he didn't know how it got there either. I remember lying in bed countless nights after that, staring up at the ceiling, listening for noises, wondering if this was the night that Dad was going to lose his mind and shoot all of us in our beds.

— — —

There was a place off Miller Run Road just west of the Adrienne River called Miller Falls. You pulled your car into a little dirt parking area and entered the woods by a footpath that descended a hundred feet to the bottom of a ravine. Then you walked two miles to a waterfall that flowed only after a great rain. If you went any other time, it was dry.

When Dad heard about this place, he immediately took us to see it. I don't remember how impressed I was with the falls. The most significant part of this experience was the walk back to the car. As we ascended this steep footpath back up out of the ravine, we were met by a gang of bikers, probably a dozen of them, all with shaggy beards and leather jackets and heavy boots and chains clanking all over. They were like a small horde of Vikings thundering toward us. I panicked. I absolutely panicked. Seized with terror, I clutched my mom's hand and wailed my lungs out. The tears rolled down my face and I screamed for our lives.

Dad nodded to the bikers, and they nodded back and said, "How ya doin'?"

And Dad said, "Good, you?"

And they said, "All right."

Meanwhile I wasn't waiting for the switchblades to come out. I had let go of Mom's hand and made a run for it. Mom came after me, and when she found me, I was huddled under the car in a fetal position praying for God to save us somehow. All I can say is, this is what happens to a six-year-old who'd already seen every Hells Angels movie ever made—and, believe me, there are a *lot* of Hells Angels movies, and they are *all bad*.

[FIVE]

My cellmate, Arnold, became intolerable sooner than I'd expected. Just because he was now right with the Holy Spirit didn't mean that he was above tormenting another human being. A guard walked by our cell one day whistling, and I said, "God, I hate it when people fucking whistle."

"Why?" Arnold asked.

"I don't know. I just hate it."

He grinned slightly, and began to whistle.

At first I thought it was a joke. I laughed. But he didn't stop. He whistled for days. I mean *for days*.

Imagine being trapped in a room with someone who will not stop whistling. Imagine trying to sleep while they whistle, trying to read while they whistle, trying to take a shit while they whistle in your face. Whistling doesn't even have to annoy you the way it does me. You could actually like the sound of whistling, and still, this kind of torture would make you want to kill yourself. My only peace was when he slept, and then I sat on my bunk and stared at him, imagining jamming a pencil into his ear. Not just imagining it—actually wondering if I would have to do it.

I did ask him to stop, but Arnold quickly found himself directly in front of me. He bellowed into my face as loud as he could, with sudden and murderous violence, "WHAT THE FUCK ARE YOU GONNA DO ABOUT IT?!"

The guy scared the hell out of me. He was fucking nuts. I backed away and sat down on my bunk, and he continued his whistling gleefully.

Finally, one day as we were being taken out to rec, I asked a guard, Leonard, if there was any way I could be put into a private cell. He nodded, as if he'd known I would at some point ask this. Before the day was through, I found myself alone, and at peace, in P-13 up on the third floor, with a window overlooking the rec yard.

[SIX]

My dad used to hunt groundhogs somewhat regularly, but I never saw him do it, until one day when I was five, I think. He shot it on the railroad tracks from a distance of about twenty yards. The thing was scurrying across the tracks as my dad took aim with what kind of rifle I don't remember, but it must have been a big one. He fired. The groundhog let out an awful squeal and stood up on its hind legs. Its entrails were hanging out. Somehow my dad had blown its stomach out. It was the most horrible thing I'd ever seen. Dad dropped the gun to his side and stood still for a moment, stunned, I think, by how awful the sight was. Then he walked to the groundhog and shot it again, killing it this time.

I don't think Dad ever seriously hunted again after that. He still kills animals, sure, but because they've invaded his property—which is still, I think, kind of insane—but he doesn't *hunt*, technically speaking—he defends. He has little holes in the screen in his bedroom window and a .22 rifle leaning against the wall. Mom yells at him for shooting from inside their bedroom, but he says he doesn't have time to go outside.

"They're too fucking fast," he says. "They're gone by the time I get out there."

Mom throws up her hands. "Then don't kill them," she says.

"But I have to! They're taking over."

She shakes her head, like she always does, seeing that it's pointless to argue.

— — —

Late one night Dad and Mom were fighting. It was a tremendous explosion of violent yelling. I was in bed, I was tiny, I didn't understand anything about anything but I understood something was completely wrong. Dad was yelling, "Then I'll just fucking leave! I'll fucking walk out that goddamn door."

I wailed like it was the end of the world. My bedroom door opened and there was Dad, in his leather motorcycle jacket with guns in his arms—several rifles—and a cigarette hanging out of his mouth. He came in. "What's wrong?" he asked. "What's wrong?"

I sat up and yelled, "You're going! You're going!"

He came over to my bed and leaned the guns against the side of it. As he bent down and kissed me on the forehead, hugged me, the ember fell off his cigarette and burned a hole in my pillowcase. He smelled like beer and smoke, and his jacket was cold and smooth.

"I'm not going anywhere," he said. And he didn't. He didn't leave.

— — —

Dad said that his teachers in high school—ninth grade was the furthest he got, so I always assumed he was talking about ninth-grade teachers—would draw pictures of him during class because he was so beautiful. His hair was perfect. Curly ringlets on his forehead in the center, sides slicked back into a ducktail at the rear. He was James Dean if James Dean was a thug. Leather motorcycle jacket and black leather railroad boots, white T-shirt and black jeans. On a summer day he'd roll his Camel filterless cigarettes up in the sleeve of his T-shirt. He had jailhouse tattoos on his arms and hands. One says GIRLS BORN TO RAISE KIDS. He said that originally the word "girls" was absent, but no one understood. He had to explain himself—this probably means he had to fight—too often, so he changed the meaning of the statement by adding that one word. Another says BORN TO LOSE.

To hear my dad's stories, and he told stories all the time—not the same stories over and over, mind you, but different ones, and when he did repeat himself, the story didn't change, so you knew he wasn't lying; it deepened, broadened, gained more dimensions, became more real and more interesting—but to listen to him briefly, you'd think that he had been nothing but a thug, a beer-drinking, fist-swinging little psychopath—at barely ninety pounds, the scrawniest and most excitable little bastard you'd ever see. Hitchhiking from his hometown in the hills to the city and back again with his brother, drunk the whole way and stopping at every bar they passed, Dad with a .38 pistol in his pocket. They met a guy who showed them a bag of money and wouldn't tell them where he got it. Dad wanted to pop the guy and dump him in the woods, take the money, but his brother talked him out of it.

I imagine them both hunched over a little table covered with empty beer bottles and cigarette ashes. Dad's eyes are gleaming with vicious excitement, but his brother's cool, relaxed.

"That's a lot of money," Dad says. "A *whole* lot of money."

"Yup." My uncle leans back in his chair and takes a swig of beer. "And they'll fry you in the electric chair."

"But, shit . . ." Dad looks back over at the guy, who's sitting at the bar. He fingers the .38 and imagines all that money; then he imagines forty thousand volts, and he shrugs off the idea.

— — —

You can hear a man repeat two different stories about doing time and get the impression that he spent more time in lockup than he did outside. You can hear him tell three stories about hitchhiking and imagine that he spent half his life on the road. He can tell you about an old couple who picked him up on a lonely road. The old lady opens the glove compartment and inside is a revolver. She says to her husband, "We gonna do this one like we did the last one?" So he leaps out of the car at the next stop sign and runs for his fucking life.

He can tell you about the time he was walking on a highway near Wheeling one night at two or three in the morning and spotted a car idling on the shoulder with its parking lights on. Another car pulls up beside it and there are gunshots, both interiors lit up by the flash of gunfire, and the second car drives off. When he gets up to the remaining car and looks in, he sees a fresh corpse with half its head missing and blood all over the place, so he takes off into the woods and sticks to the hills, in case anybody sees him.

He can tell you about the three different times that he died, clinically died, flatlined, and came back to life: once from drowning, once from bleeding to death, and once from blood poisoning. He can tell you about all the people he knew who died under truly disturbing circumstances—not the least of which was his own father, crushed by a hundred million tons of rock.

And then there was the girl who cussed like a sailor. He'd take his friends to her house—they'd walk ten miles just to hear her cuss.

He can tell you he joined the marine corps to fight in Vietnam because he thought that if he did then maybe another man, one with a wife and kids, might be spared, but he was discharged because of his bad leg. About the fights he started with his drill sergeants because he didn't like their attitudes.

You could hear a man tell you all these things, and

more, and wonder what kind of world he lived in—what other reality did he occupy where so many absurd and fantastic things happen to one man?

If he's your father, you will spend your life listening to these stories, formulating expectations of your world based on them, and soon you'll expect much more from the world than you're likely to get. And you'll learn to expect violence.

— — —

I was ten years old. Dad was in his shed building something out of wood—perhaps a little shelf or a reindeer. Mom was in there talking to him, and when I entered, I asked, "Dad, can I go out to David's for a while?" David was my best friend, lived out in the country.

Dad looked at me. He had a scowl on his face and he was dripping sweat. He was always sweating. He drank more ice water and sweated more during the summer than any man I've ever seen. "No," he said. "I've already said yes to you too many times today."

"Oh, Hank," Mom said, and he shot her a harsh look. She shut up and looked away.

Dad turned around to face me fully. "Get down on your knees," he said.

"Why?"

"Do what I say. Get down on your knees and ask me if you can go to David's."

I got down on my knees and said, "Can I go to David's?"

"No!" His eyes were wide and his face was contorted, instantly insane, the kind of expression you'd expect on a man who was about to split your head in two with an ax. "You don't get down on your knees for nobody! Get back in the house."

I burst into tears and ran into the house and up the stairs. When I got to the top of the stairs, I picked up a cassette tape that I'd left on the floor earlier, and when I entered my bedroom, half blinded by rage, I flung it at the wall, only it didn't hit the wall. It smashed through a pane of glass in my window and fell to the ground outside. I stopped. My rage turned instantly to panic. Now I was in a state of hysterics. I ran downstairs and found my mom in the living room.

"What's wrong?" she asked. But I couldn't stop to tell her. I ran outside to clean up the glass and get the tape. She followed me. She helped me clean up the glass and she hugged me. I slobbered on her blouse. I couldn't get my breath. I was terrified that Dad was going to whip me. She said, "No, go tell him what happened and apologize."

"*No!*"

"It's okay. Go ahead, he'll understand."

Five minutes later, Dad violently pushed me back into the house while struggling to undo his leather belt. "Get in the damn corner!" And he pushed me into it. I began to scream. "What are you yelling for? You want something to yell about?" And he lashed my ass with the belt.

When I think about my dad, my ass stings. Years into my adulthood, I acquired this strange muscular memory of the many ass-whippings I'd received from him when I was a kid—unjust ass-whippings. He couldn't contain himself, would laugh wildly while he swung the belt—a maniac, an insane man. I can still feel the sting. Not just a spot on one cheek, but multiple slashes on both cheeks. It's like I'm being whipped all over again, every time I remember.

[SEVEN]

As the weeks passed, I adapted. At about three months, I was capable of imagining spending the rest of my life in jail. I had grown entirely accustomed to life on the inside. I no longer thought excessively about fast food or about having sex, about anything that wasn't actually attainable. I jerked off all the time, but actually getting laid was like getting a cigarette—it just wasn't going to happen. Once I got a handle on the routine, jail was not that bad. I was amazed by how quickly I became accustomed to it. Your expectations narrow, the scope of your world extends mostly to the area right around you—sometimes down to the shower and the rec yard.

The routine was soothing.

Monday was popcorn night. Every inmate got a bag of freshly popped popcorn. It was the best popcorn I'd ever had. The trustees would push the popcorn cart around the jail and hand out the bags. Trustees were adult inmates who, for whatever reason—because of either their good behavior or the low level of their crimes—were allowed to perform duties in the jail, like cleaning or distributing food. I asked one time if I could be a trustee since at least it was something to do, but they said I couldn't because I was a juvenile.

I was segregated, kept mainly out of contact with adult inmates, because I was a juvenile and hadn't yet been convicted. I was awaiting trial. The second I was convicted, juvenile or not, I'd be thrown in with the adult population. I'd be just like any other inmate. I could maybe be a trustee then, but I was pretty sure I'd be more concerned with keeping my ass intact than with passing out popcorn.

Tuesday was commissary day. Every inmate had an account with the jail. My mom made sure I had enough cash to get the things I desperately needed, like a week's worth of Nutty Bars, pencils and pads for writing letters, a bag of foul-smelling powder that, when mixed with tap water, miraculously became fruit juice, and other necessities. I'd put in my order on Friday. On Tuesday, Mona, a mammoth lesbian guard who had a satisfying maternal quality, would deliver the merchandise straight to my cell door. She never spoke an extraneous word, but she was polite, and she never made a mistake with the commissary.

Wednesday was library day. Belinda, the wonderful librarian, who was petite and had light brown hair, brought the cart by and I could check out as many books as I liked. If I made a list of books I'd like to read, she'd take it with her and return the next Wednesday with whatever I asked for, unless I asked for things like porn or bomb-making recipes.

Thursday was laundry day. A trustee came by for my dirty laundry, and would return it on Friday. Even getting clean laundry back was an event. A garbage bag full of freshly starched white T-shirts, socks, and gray sweatpants was deposited next to my cell door. I'd spend half an hour folding them all, getting them just right. Again, it was something to do, something to make the time seem well used.

Nothing happened on the weekends.

[EIGHT]

I talk about my dad so much because he was the ground that I grew out of, and the ideal vision he had of himself as a young badass was the same ideal vision that I eventually adopted for myself. But Dad was not like anyone else's dad. Other dads seemed rock solid; they were vaults. They stood firm like buildings and they were closed off and they made no spontaneous sounds. My dad filled the room with whatever he was. He didn't hold anything back. My dad was insane. He was complicated. He had a past that was twisted and scary and his mind was twisted and scary, but he was a boy who had never found it very easy to behave like he had shit under control. He never had anything under control, the way I've never had anything under control. Just an eternal *what-the-fuck?* kind of feeling about everything.

What is it? I still struggle with a mystified half-grasp of the complexities of human motivation. I mean, there's always something more there. . . . I've never been able to just toss something into a recognizable category of behavior and say, "Well, all right, that's just the way it goes." I've never been able to pretend that it's not all really, truly, deep down and always, completely fucking astonishing in its ultimate and inescapable *weirdness*.

So there's something there. How many kids grow up with homicide as a constant topic of humor and conversation in their house? I mean *constant*. How many kids grow up with a thick, sickening paranoia snuffing out their natural pleasure and excitement for life?

My dad was always, *always* talking about what he'd do if somebody broke into the house while we were sleeping, *always* talking about why he kept a bunch of guns by the bed. I mean, I grew up assuming it was inevitable that somebody would break into the house at night to kill us. The world was full of people who wanted to kill or mutilate us.

He said, "All right, Nate, we're going to this store over here in town. Now, not too long ago a little kid like you ran off by himself and went to the bathroom alone, and some guy was in there, some fucking pervert, and you know what he did? You know what he did?"

"No."

"He took a knife and cut that boy's peepee off. He just cut it right off."

This was my first depression. I remember it. How old could I have been? Five? This was my first experience of psychotic paranoia. Sick fear. Because that was *real*, it was not hypothetical—little boys get their peepees cut off in this world. It could happen to me. It could happen to anybody.

Fear dominated my dad's sense of life. The foundation of my dad's worldview is a horror, a sick trembling in the face of overwhelming cruelty.

This he gave to me.

And we know what happens to people who are afraid, people who are scared to death, who maybe aren't able to recognize their fears, who maybe can't do anything at all about their fears. . . . They get frustrated, and eventually that frustration comes out as anger. They realize on some unconscious level that in a world where overwhelming cruelty looms constant, it'll take a pretty mean son of a bitch to come out on top. If the threat's that powerful, your response had better be at least as powerful.

So as I grew up I developed a fetish for weapons, just like my dad had. I collected knives and guns, brass knuckles, lead pipes, swords . . . anything that could kill or maim. I'd seen films where guys had arsenals in their homes, and I tried to create my own.

My dad had an arsenal. I'd stand in his arsenal, surrounded by all those guns and knives, and you know how I'd feel?

Safe.

To be safe meant being capable of doing violence, but at first this primitive understanding wasn't clearly conscious.

There was a spot in the creek that ran by our house where a huge metal pipe coated with tar ran from one bank to another. It was about a foot above the water, at the deepest point in the creek. This is where everyone swam. We referred to the spot as the Black Pipe. There was a train trestle on the other side of town, past the park where the ball diamonds were, which we always referred to as the Black Bridge. It was a sad day when it was finally removed. From then on, the spot was referred to as the Place Where the Black Bridge Used to Be. By that time, I'd ride my bike out to that spot and smoke cigarettes.

Once my friend Philip and I took Dad's .32 derringer out there and shot up a storm, pretended we were gangsters and tried to formulate some plan for taking over the town, extorting the businesses and so on. But long before this, when I was probably eight or nine, I was wandering around the bank by the Black Pipe and saw a bird playing in the sand by the edge of the water. Without thinking, I picked up a large rock and flung it at the bird. It hit it squarely in the back, probably snapped its spine, and the bird began to flop around, flap its wings, and twitch its legs. I was overcome by a feeling of dread, a sickness, and I panicked and ran away. I don't remember how long it took for me to recover from it, probably an afternoon, but an image of that poor bird, broken, flopping around in the sand, used to come back to me at times—it used to strike me for no discernable reason and bring back the sickness, the utter drenched-in-misery despair I'd felt when it happened.

In third grade I chased another boy, and as we rounded one of those huge concrete pipes we liked to climb on, I shoved him as hard as I could. He slid on the gravel and his face hit a concrete slab pretty hard—blood spread out around his face. I thought he was dead. I stood over him, mystified, horrified. I felt just like I did after I broke the bird's back. After a teacher had carried him into the school, I saw shavings of bloody skin stuck to the slab of concrete, as if it had been sanded off his face.

I went to see him in the nurse's office to tell him I was sorry, but all I could do was cry. He lay there with a bandage covering half his face, and he looked up at me as if to say, "How could you do this?"

I don't know how I could do it. I just did it.

But more killing would come, more violence, more animosity, and there was no stopping it. Kids do what they want before they know they want to, or more importantly *why* they want to, and almost always after it's too late—this is why some kids end up blind and maimed or in a persistent vegetative state. Just having a little fun, that's all. Childhood is a long dream of blood and rape, as far as I have seen, about the setting of land mines in the unconscious, the planting of fantastic future mushroom clouds, the creation and living out of insane earth religions: primitive, brutal, and simple. Innocence is a total lack of impulse control. Innocence, or the ability to stop doubting ourselves, is what we adults still long for.

[NINE]

Not long before the robbery, I had seen the Oliver Stone film *The Doors*. I had always, in a way, been into writing: horror when I was young, then rock lyrics when I got older. There was something about the poetry in that film that stuck with me, and so when one Wednesday I noticed a biography of Jim Morrison on the library cart, I checked it out. Before that, I'd been reading Stephen King, Clive Barker, some fantasy, but nothing heavy. Not to say that a bio of Morrison is *heavy*, but what it led to is another matter entirely.

Up until this point the only counterculture figures I had ever encountered or thought I understood were bikers, gang members, mobsters, and assassins. My world didn't contain intellectual rebels. My world didn't contain intellectuals, period. Granted, whether or not Morrison can actually be considered an intellectual is debatable, but he was an artist and he did read a lot, did a lot of drugs, had a lot of sex. This looked like a pretty god-damned good life to me. The most important thing the Morrison bios did for me (I read four of them) was to list the writers who had influenced him. I wrote down every one of those writers and handed the list to Belinda, who would always smile and say something like, "Good choice." Soon the greats were flowing into my cell, and I was eating them up as fast as they came. Kerouac's *On the Road*, Nietzsche's *Beyond Good and Evil*, Rimbaud's *Season in Hell*, Ginsberg's *Howl*.

I read all the Kerouac books Belinda could find. I copied *Howl* by hand onto yellow legal paper so that I could reread it again and again. Something was happening; a new world was opening up for me. I could see suddenly that a great conversation was going on, had been going on since human beings began to write, and I wanted to be a part of it. And the conversation wasn't just about what kind of jobs people had or what kind of vacations they might take, but about every aspect of human experience. These men were revolutionaries in a way that I could never have conceived before. The world was becoming deeper; whole universes of possibilities and questions were exposing themselves to me. I didn't understand Nietzsche—I could barely read him then—but I knew he was important. These were murmurings, which were becoming clamorings, of a whole reality that neither I, nor indeed anyone I had ever known, had ever even imagined. It was the beginning of thought. It was the beginning of questioning.

It was a slow process. At first, the books taught me

that I should try a lot of drugs, rush about frantically looking for something indefinable, and then fall into an intolerable depression for a long time. This was what it seemed intellectuals did. But you begin asking questions for fun, and then the questions grow into you, and they take over. You don't even know it's happening.

No longer would I be capable of taking anything for granted, accepting just anything, believing that there weren't alternatives. There were always alternatives. Factory job? Wife and kids? Living and dying in a small Indiana town? No, there were opium dens and whorehouses on the other side of the world. There were parlors where geniuses smoked pipes and debated the course of history, and there were French girls in Paris who took mushrooms and saw the secret of the universe. I wanted nothing more than to be there with them.

[TEN]

I met David in fourth grade on a field trip to Indianapolis. He asked me if he could sit with me on the bus,
and a week later I was out at his house in the country for
the night, running through the woods and discovering the
insides of wild animals, which in the beginning made
me quite sick. I remember the first time David took a
groundhog under the blade. He did it with such kid pride
in destruction and gritty country know-how, gleefully
sickening me, a boy from the city. Not that Brickville
was much of a city. There were maybe a thousand people
living there, but to David and all the kids out on the farm,
it was a fucking metropolis.

The Turner farm consisted of a moderately dilapi-
dated two-story peaked-roof house with a front porch
that had a swing on it, one ancient wooden barn with
peeling red paint near the driveway that functioned as a
garage, and a larger, newer, gray sheet-metal horse barn

next to a pasture. The house sat on a small hill, which sloped down into the horse pasture.

One snowy winter day David and I were crouched at the top of the hill. I was all wrapped in winter clothes, sitting on a plastic sled. David laid the dead animal out on the snow and, with his pocketknife, sliced its front side open from groin to mouth, exposing steaming entrails. I was nauseated, and I slid off down the hill to escape the horror.

But soon enough I was converted, and I was killing and dissecting my own beasts, gutting them, or field-dressing them, as it is called by hunters. David has always and with much pride claimed responsibility for turning me into a bloodthirsty killer. Killing made us more a part of the wilderness: killing animals was not to us anything to be ashamed of, and it was not a sport—it was a natural function.

They had a bunch of chickens out there at David's farm, and every once in a while Gladine, his mother, a God-fearing matriarch whose mouth and mind were further from the gutter than anyone I know, would tell us to go kill a chicken for dinner. How we relished this duty—it's amazing how much blood is in a chicken and how messy this job is.

We'd tie one rope to the chicken's legs and another to its neck and stretch the neck over a stump. David would belt out some kind of ninja *hi-ya!* and bring an ax down with all his might. He could usually sever the neck in one swing, and the blood would spray in every direction as the decapitated bird flopped around, not going anywhere because its legs were tied. It would be a summer day and we'd have been swimming in the creek or horseback riding, barefoot and shirtless and wearing damp shorts. Droplets of hot blood speckled our chests and reddened our feet.

— — —

Everyone at school picked on David, but it never seemed to bother him. He was a perpetual outsider. He was like a wild kid that someone had found roaming the woods on all fours, and then barely civilized him through severe punishment. His clothes were always filthy and stained with animal blood—the same clothes he hunted in. On the elementary school playground, if anyone ever asked me where David was, I'd say, "Look for the buzzards." I thought this was pretty witty.

In fourth grade David would bring severed raccoon paws to school and scratch girls with the claws. There didn't seem to be any real provocation for this. He just hated the girls. There'd be a crowd of them gathered at recess, talking, laughing; then suddenly chaos would erupt and one of the girls would go into a panic, screaming about rabies and dying. And David would run from the group waving the paw in the air like a maniac. The principal whipped him more than once for this.

I was whipped only once at school, and that was for punching another kid in second grade. I knocked the kid's tooth out. His name was Rich Bass, and to this day he has a screw-in tooth because of me. I honestly cannot remember whether it was intentional or not. I do remember how thoughtless, how fast, blurred, chaotic things were then—running and chasing, as if I'm flying a thousand miles an hour over gravel or asphalt.

— — —

Because Dad was so paranoid, so worried, so fretful about everything—and he *was* fretful, the worst possibilities always occurring to him first—I wasn't allowed to do much. Most of the time I was confined to the house. I was allowed to spend time at the Turner farm because Mom and Dad assumed I was being supervised. They assumed Gladine, being the good woman she was, kept a pretty firm grip on the actions of her six children, but she didn't. She believed that kids who live in the country should be able to roam the countryside. They should be able to camp and hunt and fish and swim, and we did all those things. We rode horses at full gallop across the fields bareback. And it *was* innocent . . . in a sense.

David and Philip and I slaughtered wild animals for fun. I've still got the severed paws of a groundhog whose head I beat to mush with brass knuckles. We got high on the killing. It seemed natural. We thought it was just like what anybody else did when they went out during deer season with a rifle. We just had more passion for it, so we figured we should do it all the time.

The woods in which we did the killing were mostly barren of life by the time we were sixteen. The dogs would tree raccoons, possums, or groundhogs, and we would stone them with heavy rocks from the railroad tracks until they fell; then we'd beat them with sticks or hatchets or hammers—we seldom took guns along, at least when we were young. We hunted with unorthodox weapons, and it was tough. Unless you're a crack shot at throwing hammers, you will never kill a squirrel with one. We once killed a groundhog with a pellet gun, shot him thirty times in the throat before I laid into him with the brass. With a hacksaw, I took my souvenirs.

One night when I was fifteen, we were camping in the horse field with great bonfires fifteen feet tall, drinking beer and smoking skunk weed through modified soda cans, and the dogs found a possum in a tree across the creek. While David had climbed the tree and was trying to beat it out with an ax handle, I impaled it with a frog gigger, which is a long pole with a spike fitted to the end, and knocked it to the ground, then pounced on it with a pocketknife. For those moments, in the frenzy of killing, I felt like the perfect predator, performing a natural and necessary function. Nothing was out of place in the world, and I was in control.

There were hundreds of such incidents. Like the time we put a possum in a fifty-gallon drum and tortured it with sharp sticks and pokers until it was seething. But torture was rare. On my sixteenth birthday, David and I went hunting with kitchen knives and a .22 rifle and we found a raccoon at the base of a walnut tree. There was a lot of brush around and the animal was trapped, so we took our time filling it with holes. Raccoons make such a terrible hissing sound while dying. That same night, a couple of miles away, we found another raccoon about twenty feet up in a tree. We could see only the reflection of our flashlight off its eye and so, naturally, that's what we aimed for. We probably wasted fifty shots and still hadn't made any progress when we realized that we were down to our last shell. David climbed the tree, his specialty, and began to poke at the beast with a twelve-inch butcher's knife. The raccoon fell on top of him and then down the tree. It was scrambling down the trunk, about five feet from the ground when I took aim. I fired, but missed. It continued to advance. I spun the rifle around and brought the butt of it down onto the raccoon's head, then again and again until there wasn't anything left.

I would eventually, many years after all this, acquire a lot of cats, tons of cats, mostly strays, and I would lavish them with affection. I would pamper my goddamn cats. I would overidentify with them, to compensate for the horrors I visited upon the animal kingdom when I was young. It wasn't just cats, it was all animals. One day I stopped my car in the middle of a road and leaped out, dodging fast cars and ignoring the assholes flipping me off and honking, so I could carry a giant turtle to safety, as it was obviously taking too long for it to cross. I'd save the lives of doomed raccoons trapped by exterminators. I would not be able to help myself on such occasions. I wouldn't *choose* to empathize with the animals—I just had such little empathy for them when I was young that, when it came years later, it would be strong and sometimes very heavy with guilt.

[ELEVEN]

Flynn knocked on my cell door at five thirty in the morning. He didn't knock very loudly—he tapped, not with his knuckles either but with the pads of his fingertips. He opened the door slowly, silencing the clank of his brass keys as much as he could, poked his face into the dark cell, and asked quietly, oh so quietly, if I wanted to go to the recreation yard or if I wanted a shower.

He was quiet for a reason. He wasn't being considerate. He just didn't want me to wake up. He didn't want me to have rec or a shower. He wanted to whisper into my cell, and he wanted me to groan, and he wanted to write on my sheet that I refused rec and shower for the day. He wanted as many guys as possible to "refuse" rec and shower—it would be less work for him.

I got to leave my cell for an hour a day. One hour out of twenty-four. The rest of the time I stayed in the cage—this was my life now—and just so that Flynn could spend more time at work doing nothing, he did everything he could to cheat me out of that one hour.

"You fucking shit," I said. "What time is it?"

Flynn huffed. "You want rec or shower or not, Henry?"

"Do I want to go outside and throw basketballs at a little hoop for half an hour before the sun has even come up, when it's thirty degrees out, when I've only had four hours of sleep?"

"Yes or no?"

"I want you to come back at a reasonable hour and ask me the same fucking question, man."

"This is your only chance, Henry. Either you take it now or you don't go."

"Fuck you," I said. "I'm going to write a grievance."

"Fuck you too," he said. "Write your grievance."

Flynn slammed the cell door shut and walked off to the next poor bastard who was in no shape to go out into the cold any more than I was, no shape to take a cold shower with that bastard staring at him the whole time.

He made his rounds at five thirty in the morning, as early as he could, when more guys were likely to still be out of it, more likely to refuse, and then he sat on his disgusting ass for the next five hours doing nothing. I hated the son of a bitch.

[TWELVE]

Brickville's most unruly children seemed to come from one neighborhood, an old apartment complex known as the Projects, even though they weren't technically housing projects at all. They were poor kids, and their parents didn't seem to give a shit where they were or what they were doing. There were two or three dozen Project boys, and quite a few of them later became my friends. But for the longest time I was not on their good side, and they took every opportunity to torment me.

One afternoon when I was eleven, Philip and I were out in a field a few miles from his house throwing rocks at an old hollowed-out tree when we decided to search a nearby shed. Hidden up in the loft of this small building was a duffel bag full of porn magazines. It's really amazing how many porn magazines we used to find, and every time it was like winning the lottery.

That evening when we came out of the shed, we

found ourselves surrounded by half a dozen Project boys, all armed with BB guns. They were led by Charlie Bender, who would remain the leader of that group for years to come; in fact, he's probably still their leader. They ordered us to raise our hands, and we did. They marched us out of the field, but just before we got to the road, Charlie snickered and shot me in the ass. I yelped and began to cry as quietly as I could. I was terrified.

Charlie said, genuinely concerned, "Man, what's wrong? We're just fucking with you."

"I don't know," I said. "I've just seen too many war movies, I guess."

That night, back at Philip's house, Amy was hanging around and I asked her to look at my ass. There was a group of girls who lived down the road. Their dad was an out-of-work drunk, and their mother was dead, so they were always running wild—we called them the crazy girls, because they were, or at least they seemed to be. Amy was the oldest of crazy girls, slightly younger than me, and I had a mild crush on her from the beginning, but this crush would later grow into a full-blown obsession.

"*What?*" she said.

"Will you look at my butt? I got shot. Tell me if I need surgery."

"That's disgusting."

"Please."

"All right."

I unbuttoned my pants and moved them down past my ass cheek, and she examined it closely. This was incredibly thrilling. It was worth being shot in the ass to have Amy look at my ass.

"There's a welt," she said.

"A welt? What's a welt?"

"A bump."

I turned back around to face her and buttoned my pants. She had long brown hair and hazel eyes. I wanted to touch her.

"A bump?" I asked.

She laughed and said, "You're stupid." And she ran out of the house screaming, "STUPID! STUPID! STUPID!"

— — —

There was one Project boy who was particularly evil. His name was Random Cordero and he was a complete bastard. There was nothing redeeming about him. He was bigger than everybody and bullied anyone who wasn't a part of his clan. One evening when I was riding my bike home from Philip and David's house, just when I entered town, he appeared out of nowhere and began to chase me. I panicked and pedaled as fast as I could. He stayed right on my ass the whole way home.

He kept yelling, "I'm gonna get you, you fucker!"

I pedaled straight into our carport and crashed into the fence. He just kept on riding. A couple of weeks later I was fooling around under the bridge and he showed up. He didn't say a word. He just tripped me and stepped on my chest. I was in the mud and he pressed his foot into the middle of my chest, pushing the wind out of me.

I couldn't breathe. He just grinned like a fucking psychopath. I began to panic, and just then my mother yelled for me. He let me go and I ran like hell.

Not too long after this, Random got himself a job at a Pizza Hut in Beckettstown and started dating a girl. The girl had previously been involved with a black dude, and this black dude was a mean son of a bitch. Random ran his mouth off to the guy, probably called him all sorts of racist shit, and one night when Random was taking the trash to the Dumpster, the black dude got ahold of him. It wasn't very late in the evening and the area around Pizza Hut is pretty busy. There were lots of people around, lots of spectators. They watched this guy stomp Random to death, right there in the parking lot of Pizza Hut.

I heard about it from Random's uncle while I delivered ads on a Sunday morning. I was disturbed inasmuch as any fatal beating will be disturbing, but to be honest, as for Random being dead, I did not feel terribly bad.

[THIRTEEN]

I was in P-13 for maybe a month. I grew used to being alone. I slept for as long as I needed to and was always fully rested. I read a great deal, always had a stack of books a foot and a half high by the head of my bunk. This stack of books served as an end table on which I could rest my coffee while reading. I'd read for hours and hours at a stretch. I'd finish a five-hundred-page book in just a couple of days. I even started writing poetry. It rhymed, and since I used a dictionary and a thesaurus, my vocabulary was growing exponentially. I couldn't pronounce a huge percentage of those words because I'd never heard them spoken aloud, but I knew what they meant.

The meals were bad, but I got used to them. There's a thin slot about two feet up from the bottom of the cell door—this slot has its own steel door on hinges, which opens outward and downward to form a kind of shelf on which the trustees set your food tray. When the guard unlocks the tray door and slams it down, it racks the cell with noise. They came with breakfast at six o'clock in the morning when I was down in P-1. In P-13 it came at around six forty-five. With oats, toast, and a hard-boiled egg, we had a choice of awful watery lukewarm milk, mixed in vats with water and dried concentrate, or coffee. I began to opt for the coffee. It was awful shit at first. I don't know anyone who ever loved coffee from the start, but I grew to love it and began to order bags of instant coffee through commissary. I drank it constantly.

My cell overlooked the rec yard, so I'd watch my fellow inmates when they were out there. Most of them were comfortable in this environment. They ranged from young thugs to old men. Most of them had been to prison before and knew what sort of behaviors and attitudes to adopt. They puffed out their chests and strutted, sometimes pumping their fists outward for no apparent reason, as if delivering a punch. I didn't want to go to prison with these fuckers.

My public defender, the one time I talked to him, didn't offer any reason to be optimistic. All he would say is, "We'll do what we can do." Then he began to request continuance after continuance, which are postponements of trial. He told my parents that I was better off where I was, rather than home on bail, because by the time I went to trial, I would have already served a percentage of whatever was likely to be my sentence. But bail was not a possibility anyway. Besides, I had been on probation in Indiana, and there were charges against me for stealing Dad's gun and car and skipping probation. If they bailed me out, I'd just be arrested again as soon as I got home. So either way I was screwed.

My public defender wouldn't offer any guesses as to how much time I might get, and he didn't give me any cause for optimism, so as far as I knew, I was eventually going to end up mixed in with those barbarians down there strutting their shit in the rec yard. It was just something I was going to face.

There's a difference between county jail and prison. If you've committed a felony—like murder or armed robbery—you go to county to await your trial, and if you get a long sentence, you're shipped off to prison. If you've committed a misdemeanor, maybe you'll do a couple of months in county and that's it. A lot of convicts who've been through county jail and to prison will tell you they'd rather be in prison any day of the week. You can't smoke in county, it's harder to smuggle dope into county, and there's limited movement around the facility. Prison is penitentiary. Think San Quentin. Think guard towers and guards with machine guns. They house hundreds, if not thousands, of inmates. County jails usually house at most only a few hundred inmates. They're smaller and—I'm going to guess, since the population is more transient—less corrupt when it comes to smuggling contraband, and you can't smoke.

Prisons are huge, civilizations within themselves, and the populations are sorted out by race or by gang. If you're used to this sort of thing and you're a hard-core thug, maybe it's no big deal—who knows? Maybe if I were up in a cell block with a bunch of thugs, I'd feel differently, but I wasn't—I was kept by myself or sometimes with other juvies, and that was fine by me. I'd rather just be left alone to read my books. But it wasn't going to stay that way forever—when I was finally sentenced, finally convicted, I would sure as hell be sent to prison. No more books. No more quiet contemplation. Into the fucking jungle I'd go. I'd get my ass kicked, I'd get fucked in the ass, I'd get a makeshift knife in the kidney, and there I'd die. I was positive.

This threat of real prison was not easy on my parents. For the time being, they knew I was safe, but no mother wants to imagine her boy raped or beaten. And for years after all this, my dad actually left the room when the subject arose. Once I cried on the phone with Mom. I was sitting on the floor with my back against my cell door, with a knee up, middle of the day, sun streaming in through the window. A crowd of barbarians was being herded down the corridor and one of the punks unplugged my phone. The phone cord ran under the door and out into the hallway, where it connected with a jack near the floor, and some shit thought it'd be a cute thing to do to just unplug it.

I leaped to my feet and kicked and punched the door and shouted. I screamed every threat I could come up with. All I heard was that snickering—the stupid laughter only a bully can produce. I banged on the door until my hands hurt and my voice was raw. Then I collapsed, and wept.

Pretty soon Josh came by my door and said, "Your phone's unplugged. You want me to plug it back in?"

I got up and sniffed, and said, "Yeah, thanks, man."

Most of the time, though, I held up fine. On their way to visit me, my parents and my brother, while winding down the corridors to my cell, passed dozens of other cells, and dozens of other visitors. Dad said a lot of them turned his stomach, the way those guys whined and cried. My dad said he didn't want to think about how other men behaved in that situation. And one time he said, "The way you're holding yourself up, Nate"—he nodded— "I'm proud."

[FOURTEEN]

I was thirteen. I stood in front of the full-length mirror in my mom and dad's room admiring myself. I wore all camouflage, combat boots, black face paint; I had a long knife hanging at my side. I had pistols shoved into my belt and a rifle in each hand. I was a mercenary. I was a soldier of fortune. I had seen action in all the remotest and deadliest parts of the world. I'd seen horrors and perpetrated atrocities that would cause a normal civilian to puke. I'd decapitated villagers. I'd seen my buddies tied to mules and pulled limb from limb, urged on by our sadistic enemies. I had endured torture. I had been to hell and back, and had the scars to prove it. An AK-47 round had gone clean through my left thigh. My right arm had nearly been severed by the blast of a land mine. My right eye squinted constantly due to a head injury sustained in a chopper crash in Cambodia. My torso was peppered with tiny round scars from a shotgun blast at close range. I had endured the worst anyone can imagine, and lived. I was so tough now, I could kill a man with my pinky toe. I was the hardest motherfucker who had *ever lived*.

I swooned inside at how powerful I looked. Right now, armed like this, dressed like this, I looked like Death. I looked like I owned the world.

— — —

David and Philip and I would suit up in our paramilitary uniforms, our faces painted green and black, and carry out missions in Brickville and the surrounding area. We'd hike into town in the dead of night, belly-crawl through ditches, and move breathless in the shadows, behind hedges, and between parked cars. These missions mostly consisted of busting out windows or slashing tires or shooting out streetlamps with pellet guns. They were weak and ineffective and brought us no glory.

Long before I set the school on fire and long before Philip and I robbed that place and made our desperate run from the cops, we were laying the foundations for such extravagance—of course, as it always is, our fantasies far exceeded reality.

The missions we had planned for the future were something else entirely. These could at least more accurately be called terrorism. There was a girl at school with wealthy parents, and we all hated her. So we made extensive plans to kidnap her and hold her for ransom, then possibly execute her.

"I say we take the money and blow her fucking head off anyway," I said.

Philip got excited. "Let's kill her parents too!"

"No," David intervened. "Murder rap's too heavy," he said. "Let's stick with the ransom plan."

Grudgingly, we agreed.

We had plans to attack our school and slaughter our fellow students. The media seems so surprised that kids are actually doing this these days. It's surprising to me that Columbine didn't happen sooner.

Our group, our American defense/terrorist organization, was called the Black Hawks. There were three hard-core members—myself, Philip, and David. We had a few reserve members, but none of them ever went on real missions. They were mostly involved in building forts and strongholds, or they took part in our drills (pellet-gun fights) and practice maneuvers.

Everything we did was a Black Hawks mission, from beating up a kid at school to stealing a pack of cigarettes to breaking into the house down the road. During its heyday our organization consumed about 99 percent of our mental and 75 percent of our physical activity.

We had a manual, written by yours truly, the Supreme Commander of Operations. It detailed our purpose, our code of conduct, how a member might advance in rank, etc. We spent most of our spare time conducting drills in the woods and fields around the farmhouse, learning how to maneuver through the rough without being detected, how to ambush, how to attack without warning, how to tolerate lying facedown in the mud or sitting in great discomfort at the top of a tree for hours. We were dedicated. We were obsessed. We were making ourselves into soldiers, into killing machines.

[FIFTEEN]

In the middle of the night, my cell door opened and a guard, Kline, said, "You want a butt buddy, Henry? I mean, a cellmate?"

I put down my coffee and my copy of *In Cold Blood* and sat up on my bunk.

"Who is it?" I asked.

"Burglary," Kline said, and shrugged. "Pissant."

"Okay," I said. So I put all my things in my big gray plastic tub, rolled up my plastic-coated mattress and sheets and thin blanket, and put it all in the shopping cart the guard had in the hallway. And off we were, back to P-1.

My new cellmate's name was Mo. He was seventeen, with hairy arms and lines on his face that at first glance looked like wrinkles, but it turned out they were scars from a pipe bomb that had blown up in his face years ago. So for a paranoid moment, I wondered if Kline had just thrown me in with a forty-year-old, set me up to be somebody's bitch, but the fear passed quickly. Mo was slightly shorter than me but stocky—powerfully built. He got up and shook my hand. I could tell that, in spite of his appearance of strength and his crude features, he was nervous.

"It's not that fucking bad in here, man," I said. "You get used to it."

He nodded and sat back down. "Yeah," he said. "You always get used to it."

I got my shit set up, the bed rolled out and made, my books spread around, my laundry under the bunk. I looked at Mo. He was sitting on his bunk, elbows on his knees, and when I turned, I saw him look up from the floor.

"How long you been in here?" he asked.

I thought for a second. "Fifty-nine days."

He nodded his head.

Mo ended up being a decent enough guy. We traded stories.

He'd carried a gun almost everywhere he went on the outside. He said he was just lucky when he got caught—it was one of the rare days when he didn't have it with him.

I asked, "What kind of gun?"

He said, "I don't know, man, a little .32. I had a Glock once but I traded it for four grams of speed."

What a fucking waste, I thought. Mo didn't love guns, obviously. Too crude to appreciate a fine piece of machinery.

"Four bags of dope for a motherfucking Glock," I said, and lay down on my bunk. "You should've stuck the guy up, taken his fucking dope, and still had your Glock."

Mo shook his head. "He was a friend of mine, man."

— — —

As I've said, my dad *always* had a lot of guns around. He even managed, at one time, to get his hands on a sawed-off rifle of some kind, all the markings and serial numbers filed off. He showed it to his friends and called it his mafia gun. Because Dad knew a lot of shady characters in Plantation, and because those shady characters knew a lot of other shady characters in Indianapolis, which was only a twenty-minute drive away, Dad got into trading guns. He didn't do anything illegal. He didn't do it to make money. He did it because he loved guns. Guns and porn, those were my dad's two great passions.

Dad had tons of pornography. Although I do remember him buying it occasionally—he'd take me to the porn shops with him—he seems to have amassed his collection by picking up magazines from the road. Hundreds of times while driving on country roads, he'd see something out of the corner of his eye, lock up the brakes and leap out, get back in with a porn magazine that someone had discarded.

"Son," he told me, "there's a lot of pussy-whipped weasels out there whose wives won't let them have this shit, so they buy it after work, jerk off on their drive home, and toss it to the birds. It's good for us—we get free porn, but I don't ever want to see you turn into a pussy-whipped weasel like that. You ever let a woman walk all over you and I'll shoot you myself."

Yes, an odd thing to tell your child.

I used to break into Dad's den to get to those magazines. I learned how to pick locks specifically for that purpose. He had millions of them but never gave me any, not until years later. He had a photo album that contained cutouts of all his favorite naked women, and it was a foot thick, a massive tome like one of the Great Books of human history, like the Bible. When I opened it, I heard trumpets and felt the kisses of pale blond seraphim upon my ears.

Now, lying on my bunk waiting for Mo to fall asleep, I often recalled that tome of Dad's with longing. I missed the solitary days of P-13 when I could jerk off any damned time I wanted. The only porn I had now was a swimsuit edition of *Sports Illustrated*, and given my starvation, that was one hell of a find. I treasured that thing. It always surprises me how secretive guys can be about masturbating. I never once heard any of my cellmates doing it and I'm fairly certain that none of them ever heard me, but Mo was a pretty quiet guy anyway.

After Arnold, I bunked with no more crazies. This was not out of choice—I didn't screen potential cellmates with personality tests, although that would have been helpful. No, after you've been alone for a couple of months, no matter how tolerable, or even sometimes enjoyable, the solitude might be, the change-up of getting a cellmate is always exciting. To be honest, the kids I met in the joint (other segregated juveniles) were generally no different than any of the other kids I'd known before, except for their chronic tendency to commit felonies. At the very least, what separated us from those kids on the outside was our misfortune in getting caught.

Arnold did serve his purpose. I used him as a high-water mark for judging the sanity of anyone I met for years to come. I have since been widely educated in the extremes of mental instability, but the Arnold Standard still holds true—whether it's about some guy at a party, a drug dealer, or a friend of a relative. Mo, for instance, was infinitely saner than Arnold. He was thoughtful— uneducated, but thoughtful. What little he did know about the world made an impression on him. He had, I suppose, something like what I had, and my brother has: the framework, the *machinery* for great intelligence. I don't mean common sense. That's nothing more than a human being's basic capacity to remember painful experiences and, to some degree, avoid them in the future.

I thought about Arnold, how he'd get by with his brutal common sense. Not long after Arnold and I were separated, he turned eighteen and was sent to a cell block. I'd watched him out in the rec yard a few times, playing with the other grown-up apes. He fit right in, I thought, except for his ridiculous blond Afro.

[SIXTEEN]

All day we Black Hawks roamed the woods and killed animals, dressed in camouflage, our rogue paramilitary uniforms mismatched from garage sales, flea markets, and surplus stores, our weapons either hatchets, brass knuckles, hunting knives, or pellet guns. When we meant business, when the day called for real blood, mass quantities of blood, and the black clouds rumbled for the sacrifice of whole populations of innocent creatures, we had .22 rifles. Mine had a scope and a ten-shot magazine, bolt action. Philip's was a single-shot bolt action or a pearl-handled pistol—the pistol he later took with us on the night of the robbery—and David joined us with his giant, brutal, murderous 20-gauge pump shotgun.

After a day like that, we'd pay a visit to the crazy girls from up the road—they'd invariably be hanging out in their barn, engaging in whatever weird rituals they engaged in. We'd storm the barn and attack them.

We'd invade with war cries and secret, not very innocent, barely realized lust. We pointed our guns at the girls' heads menacingly, spitting and ordering with such aggression— the very village-burning aggression we'd seen in those Vietnam War movies.

"Get down on the floor! Up against the wall! Don't fucking move! Don't move or I'll blow your fucking head off!"

And the girls cowered and trembled and sometimes called our bluff by smacking us, so we'd have to harshly bring down upon them the full force of our intentions. We pushed the gun barrels all the more roughly into their scalps. We tightened our grips on handfuls of hair, jerking them back as emphatic silencers—and generally it worked. Only when they had become thoroughly convinced that we were not role-playing, that we were not just *pretending*—only when they fully accepted and understood that since the time they had last seen us we had in fact *become* enemy soldiers and they were now, whether it was fair or not, whether it pleased them or not, our prisoners, and we owned them—only then would we let go. We'd kiss them, smack them on their asses, and laugh. Then we'd go back to the Turner house, up to the boys' bedroom, and change back into civilians.

The girls teased us all the time. It was an elaborate sadomasochistic drama. They came around constantly. They sought us out. They fucked with us.

We were in the doorway of the horse barn smoking cigarettes Philip had stolen from his dad when suddenly the crazy girls were all out in the front yard, about a hundred feet away, lined up and yelling at us.

"What the fuck are they doing?" I asked.

Philip shrugged. David spat.

"Being cunts," David said.

We could see them clearly from where we were, and they were lifting their shirts, showing us their breasts. Their ages ranged from eight to fourteen, so the breasts ranged from nonexistent to almost fully developed. We were shocked. None of us knew what to do.

"They're fucking insane," David said.

I couldn't take it. This was the most beautiful thing I'd ever seen in my life. Swept up in a powerful surge, I rushed out in front of the other boys and dropped my pants, a pair of baggy blue jeans that were too large for me anyway. They fell down around my ankles. I flashed them, jumped up and down, and grabbed my balls, then ran back into the barn. The girls were going crazy, laughing and screaming. Annette, twelve and a half years old, got out in front of the group and mooned us. Then the other girls noticed and pulled her back out of sight.

It was all too much. We were completely out of our minds—our raging adolescent hard-ons wanted to stab the world to death.

Philip was screaming, "I'm gonna fuck every last one of you bitches!"

Now they were growing even braver, thanks to Annette. They were all mooning us by pulling their pants down, some leaving their panties on and some not, and shaking their butts at us.

When the tension became unbearable, the girls seemed to sense it, and they ran from the yard as fast as they could. We knew instinctively that a chase was not what they wanted. They were not attempting to lure us— they never intended for us to pursue. They were just playing.

It didn't matter.

I didn't care. I didn't know what to do. So when the front door to the house slammed shut behind the last little ass, I fell back into the barn. I ignored the other boys, and I just went to jerking off, feverishly, like I was working myself to death to hold on to something that would be gone forever if I waited one second too long.

[SEVENTEEN]

My new cellmate, it turned out, was a member of a gang. A fairly well-known national gang, in fact. Mo had joined up while serving six months in a boys' reformatory in Chicago. He was well versed in the lore of the gang, knew all the signs and symbols, all the ranks, who the founders were.

I've always been fascinated by gangs. What interested me about joining a gang, and the only reason I would actually do so, was the idea of scheming my way to the top and running the whole show. I wasn't interested in being anybody's patsy or bitch.

The more I talked to Mo about this, the more I was tempted to join up. He said he knew only a few guys, three or four, in Thompsonville—the city our jail was in—who were members. He said there were a lot in Chicago, but his only connections were with the kids he'd met in the boys' reformatory. These gangs were like franchises, like small mafia crews that shook down a specific locale and sometimes had to kick a cut up to a more powerful crew. This is what I gathered. For the handful of white boys who actually joined these gangs, learned all the lingo, and went back home to fly their colors in rinky-dink little Midwestern towns, there wasn't much association at all with the larger, more serious, more vicious chapters in bigger cities.

You could, if you were ambitious enough, join up and appropriate all the knowledge you gained from the one who initiated you—because this information is passed along purely by word of mouth, and, believe me, the consistency of accuracy is astounding—then take the whole institution home with you and recruit a bunch of your own thugs. What a cinch. The gang has plenty of name recognition—every thug has heard of it—and the rules and protocols are so esoteric and idiosyncratic that no single individual could just make the shit up, so you've automatically got enough legitimacy to throw together, in a matter of months, a fully functional organized-crime ring. I was sold. My youthful dreams of power, of rulership, might just come true after all. I could be a fucking godfather.

So Mo explained the joining up process to me. It was not a pleasant prospect, but what the hell. I'd have to be beaten in—he'd punch me in the chest fifty times, as hard as he could, and I'd have to stand straight with my hands behind my back and take every single blow as fast as he could deliver them, without my backing off or falling down.

When you're in jail—I feel that I have to stress this point from time to time—you really have *nothing* to do, so no matter how idiotic an idea might actually be, it'll probably sound pretty good. Any diversion is welcome. So I said, "All right, let's do it."

I stood up against the wall with my hands behind my back. He stood in front of me, his feet firmly planted, and, with ceremonial solemnity, proceeded to pummel the shit out of me. He didn't hold anything back. Every time a fist crashed into me, a bit of breath was pushed out of my lungs. He got tired halfway through and had to take a break. The bruises were already starting to form. By the time he was done, I couldn't breathe, and neither could he.

He panted and said, "All right, brother, you're in now." He hugged me. "Welcome to the family."

I managed to wheeze something that sounded like, "Okay, thanks." I lay down on my bunk, crossed my arms over my chest, and waited for my heart to start beating again.

After the brutal beat-in, Mo presented me with a stack of college-ruled notebook paper bound by the cover of a *National Geographic* magazine. This was, as he put it, the Bible.

When he handed it to me, he said, "That's yours, brother, but if you ever show that thing to a civilian, you're a dead motherfucker."

"No problem, dude," I said. I flipped through the pages, which were covered with diagrams and symbols, listings of ranks and slang, lists of affiliated gangs and enemy gangs along with their colors and symbols. There was even a secret alphabet, and special numeric codes for giving orders, and code sounds, like birdcalls you could utter if you needed help from a brother or if you were announcing a beat-down (not to be confused with a beat-in).

Occasionally Mo would lie in his bunk and dream about us riding high in a school bus with gang symbols spray-painted all over it, armed to the teeth with machine guns and rocket launchers, all the way out to the West Coast, where we'd hook up with the original gangsters, the hardest of the hard-core. We'd be doing real gangster shit, like drive-bys or crack dealing or running a stable of hos, or all three—rock-slinging, bitch-smacking, pimped-out badass motherfuckers blasting whole neighborhoods to rubble. I occasionally indulged in these fantasies with him, just to pass the time, just to make him happy, to keep him believing that I wasn't just going to exploit the image of his beloved gang.

A day or so after Mo initiated me, a guard spotted my bruises. Evans was a squat little middle-aged guard who had a mustache and never smiled. He took us to the showers, and when I took my shirt off, he asked, "Where'd you get all those bruises?"

I said, "I fell down."

He nodded.

Evans was a man who'd seen it all, so I asked him one day, "Do guys really get raped in prison?"

"Sure, happens all the time," he said. "But those guys are pussies. They're afraid. You won't get fucked, man. They want you to just give it up. You'll fight. They'll beat the shit out of you every day, but you won't get fucked. You got heart."

[EIGHTEEN]

David went out of state with my family one year to visit our relatives on Dad's side of the family. I always loved going there, a small, economically depressed industrial city in the Appalachian hills. We'd go a couple times a year, and Mom and Dad would let me do anything I damn well pleased. At home they could be suffocating, but there, in Dad's hometown, they took the leash off.

I was probably fifteen, and I owned two leather jackets. One was your average black motorcycle jacket; the other was similar but made of cracked and peeling leather, and on the back was an image of a dagger with a bunch of roses wrapped around it. I gave David the one with roses on the back and I wore the other one. We wandered that town in style, strutted down the streets, talked about picking fights, picking up women, getting fucked up.

I said to David, "Damn, we look good in these jackets. If we don't get laid in these jackets, I'll be surprised."

David shrugged.

"I'm serious, dude." I punched him on the shoulder. "We're fucking badasses."

David was never as optimistic as me, not when it came to getting laid. He complained all day about how hot it was in his jacket. He'd say, "It's ninety degrees out here. I'm fucking dying, man."

"It's for pussy, dude. It's worth the sacrifice."

It was indeed ninety degrees out and we looked like dumbasses, walking around in the dead of summer in leather jackets just to look cool. The inside of my jacket was soaked with sweat and I was starting to stink.

"Maybe it *is* too hot," I said, and David started to slip out of his jacket when we heard a voice from a second-story window. We were walking down the main drag, but there weren't many people around. Above a music store, perched in an open window, was a young guy in his late teens wearing a white T-shirt and a baseball cap.

He said, "Hey, dudes!"

We stopped and looked up at him. "Where you from?" he asked.

We both answered at the same time. "Indiana."

"Where in Indiana?"

"Other side of Indianapolis," I said.

He nodded his head and took a hit from his cigarette. "You dudes look pretty cool. I like your jackets."

I felt a surge of pride. I grinned. I yelled, "Thanks, man!"

The guy waved, I waved, David waved, and we walked on. We *strutted* on, and our jackets stayed right where they were.

"See, man! We're fucking cool!"

"Yeah, dude," David said. "I guess we are."

We lit cigarettes and cruised.

At some point, we crossed a little bridge and David suggested we go down underneath and see if we could find frogs. I thought this was a dumb idea, but I followed him anyway. I wasn't tooling around in a black leather jacket on a hot summer day to kill frogs—I was looking to get *laid*. The bridge crossed a wide, shallow creek, and when we got underneath, David began to wade into the water, flipping over rocks, skipping stones, generally exploring. I sat down on the sandy shore and smoked a cigarette. We were not allowed to smoke yet, so we had to sneak them. The smoke we'd had on the main drag, the totally exposed broad daylight smoke, was for the benefit of our second-story admirer, and if any of my relatives had driven by just then, we'd have been screwed.

I looked around and spotted something tucked up in the girders beneath the bridge—it was brown, and looked to be made of cloth. "David, what's that?" I pointed and he investigated.

"It's a duffel bag," he said as he pulled it down. "It's heavy, too." He laid it on the ground between us and unzipped it. "*Oh, my God!*" he screamed.

"Holy shit!" I yelled. My heart almost stopped; then it began to beat like a .50 caliber machine gun. "Porn!" It was *completely full* of hard-core porn magazines. It was unbelievable. We *couldn't* have stumbled on a better find. We sat under there for two hours, examined every single page in every single magazine, and when we came up from under the bridge, we could barely walk.

"Jesus," he said. "This is a great town."

"I know. It's the greatest fucking town in the world."

We put our jackets back on and stumbled forward.

Then: "*Hey!*" It was a chick's voice. We looked around. Up the hill and just inside an apartment complex was a group of girls, teenage girls. They were hanging around on someone's porch. Finally, I thought, we're going to get laid.

I started toward them, but David said, "Dude, wait a minute."

One of the girls, a fat one, yelled, "You guys are stupid!"

I stopped dead in my tracks. What did she just say?

She yelled it again. "You guys are stupid! Only fucking geeks would wear leather jackets on a day like this. You're just trying to look cool! Faggots!"

David had already begun to walk away, quickly.

I gave the bitches the finger and a "*Fuck you!*" as loud as I could and caught up to David.

"We *are* goddamn geeks," he said. He took off his jacket and threw it at me. "I hate that jacket anyway." And he walked faster.

"Fuck those bitches," I said. But I was just as

82

humiliated. I was nauseated. I couldn't imagine anything worse than what had just happened to us. The day was ruined. Our lives were ruined.

"I hate this town," David said, and I silently agreed with him.

[NINETEEN]

There was a needle-and-ink tattoo on Mo's outer thigh that said PUSSY in huge block lettering, which he'd had a friend do when he was fourteen. When he wore shorts or got ready for a shower, it was the most glaringly obvious thing in the world.

Mo pulled the eraser out of a pencil, squeezed the metal end together, and scraped it on the floor until it was practically razor sharp. I looked up from my book occasionally and watched his progress.

When he was finished, he said, "I want you to do me a favor."

"What's that?" I asked.

"I want you to cut this fucking tattoo out of me." He pulled up the leg of his shorts and showed me the PUSSY tattoo. "I go to prison with a tattoo that says PUSSY, and I'm fucked, man."

I stared at him for a minute. Of course I recognized

what a messy job this was going to be, and the pain was just going to be too much for him to bear.

"All right," I said, and sat up. He sat down on my bunk beside me and handed me the pencil. He stared straight ahead, gritting his teeth, preparing himself. I started to scrape. Every time I scraped, the metal went in a few millimeters deeper. He winced, and pretty soon the blood was flowing down his leg onto the bunk. It was pretty clear to him and me both that if we actually succeeded in erasing the tattoo, his leg would have to be amputated.

"Fuck it," he said. "Never mind." He got a wad of toilet paper, held it against the bleeding gash. He shook his head, terribly disappointed. "Fucking PUSSY," he said. "What was I thinking?"

Not long after this attempt at jailhouse plastic surgery, Mo was bailed out. Just before he left, he gave me a powerful hug and said, "So long, brother."

"So long," I said.

He threw up a gang sign and I did the same.

"Take care, my man."

"You too." And I never saw him again.

Back to P-13, back to my books, my coffee, and my solitude.

[TWENTY]

In the great pursuit of women, of love, of the only thing that matters to a young guy—sex—there will be failure. Nobody starts out a stud, and if they do, they're a freak. Born studs are psychopathic freaks of nature, hated and envied by the rest of us. I think I saw a statistic once that said 90 percent of the single women in the world are fucked by 2 percent of the single men. I believe it. There are guys to whom this comes naturally. But to the rest of us, females are black holes of mind-crushing unpredictability, with an infinite capacity for cruelty—a necessity and a disease.

When I was thirteen or fourteen, I became obsessed with Amy, the oldest of the crazy girls from down the road.

Amy was my first addiction—I'd twist around in bed at night, a writhing junkie, unable to sleep, consumed by a need for her. Amy, the brown-eyed farm girl, never wore makeup or stockings or anything but jeans and T-shirts and tennis shoes, her dirty blond hair cut short and styled sexy, wavy, with bangs. I'm on my knees, subjugated to her—she dominates my entire world between the ages of thirteen and fifteen.

Amy would talk to me about her family, and then later about some guy she'd met who had a van . . . and what they'd do in that van. All the while I'd be wondering if she was enjoying hurting me. Of course she was. She was fifteen and had nice little tits. David and Philip and I would grab her tits, yell "Fried green tomatoes!" and run away before she smacked us.

I never made love to Amy—she kissed me once, just to make sure that I didn't stop thinking I needed her. It was my first kiss, my first sinking into another human being, with tongue and all, and for a moment—for two or three seconds—I lost myself entirely. It was my first real drug experience. But it never happened again with her.

In the creek, after a rain, a major rain, when the water got about eight feet deep down under the train trestle, the spot where it was easiest to enter the water, we were floating around and I was holding on to her and her cheek was pressed against mine. Her wet cheek, her wet hair—my God, I would've done anything to make love to her, to pull her off into the woods, behind a tree or into some deep grass and take that bathing suit off her. The bathing suit had some animal print on it, not a leopard print, maybe yellow tiger, a one-piece suit.

Eventually all the crazy girls moved—their dad had found work in another state, or something like that, and it just happened one day—they were gone. So that's how my first addiction ended—cold turkey.

[TWENTY-ONE]

A couple of preachers came to my cell one evening and asked if they could speak with me about the Word. Apparently it was their mission to save sinners like myself, so I let them come in and have a seat on my bunk while I leaned against my sink. I spent a lot of time leaning against my sink, whether someone was in my cell or not. I had to wear sweatpants all the time, and they had no pockets, so my hands would invariably find their way inside my pants, where they would lazily and soothingly fondle my balls. I found myself doing this while one of the preachers was in the middle of some sermon about why Jesus liked criminals, and why he was down with losers, whores, and poor people in general. He stopped and looked down at my pants.

I said, "I don't have any pockets. Go on."

The preacher was a young guy, maybe thirty-five, with pasty, oily, fishy-looking skin and big glasses and thin hair. His partner was just as repugnant. It seemed to me that religion often sucks these losers in and gives them a sense of purpose. I asked the preacher why, if God was all-powerful and all-knowing, did he allow any of this horror in the world to happen. It's an old question, but I liked watching them squirm. None of these weasels ever have a real answer for this. Eventually I told them I had to get back to my reading, and so they left. I'm sure they felt that if they'd just tried a little harder, they could have saved me.

— — —

I remember one time when we were pretty young, maybe nine or ten, Philip and David and I were waiting for some friends of their family, Kenny and Percella, to show up at their house. We were all going to the beach and they were running late. We were dying to go to the beach, and so we were all petrified that they weren't going to show and we were going to get fucked out of a day of aquatic pleasure. David suggested we pray.

Now, Gladine, their mom, was an incredibly religious woman, a wonderful woman in all other respects but still very religious. For a long time she forced her kids to go to church with her—and she attended some kind of horrifyingly primitive Baptist church where suddenly, for no apparent reason, people in the room would leap to their feet and start spewing nonsense, I mean literal nonsense, word salad, grunts and squeals and blubbering. They called this speaking in tongues. They believed that this was the voice of the Holy Spirit channeled through their bodies. First time I went with them, it scared the piss out of me. I mean, these were grown adults, acting like retarded children throwing tantrums. So Gladine was serious about her Jesus, and when we were very young, so was David, for at least a little while. I accepted what he told me about it, but it's this specific instance on the beach day that really sticks in my mind as the moment I first very clearly questioned the logic and sanity of prayer.

David said, "Okay, now get down on your knees and put your hands together and close your eyes."

We all did it, right out there in the driveway. If Gladine saw us from the living room window, she probably wept with pride.

David went on. "Now make sure you ask God for forgiveness of your sins first, or it won't work."

So I did that. I thought, "God, forgive me of my sins."

"Now," David said, "ask Him to make Kenny and Percella get here soon."

I thought, "God, please make Kenny and Percella get here soon." And I imagined it happening. I imagined opening my eyes and seeing them pull into the driveway. I imagined God performing a miracle. I imagined that if we had not prayed, they'd still be fifty miles away, stuck in traffic, surrounded by other cars. Then they'd disappear from the traffic and rematerialize in the driveway. I imagined that all the people they were stuck in traffic with would have to have their memories wiped clean, because after all they had just witnessed the inexplicable vanishing of an automobile. Kenny and Percella would have to have their memories wiped clean too. And the vehicle, transported through time and space like that—would it affect the atoms in the air, among other things? How would you transport something like that with people in it instantaneously? How could that happen? How could you do something like that? And why would he do it for us? Just because three kids want to go to the beach. There are billions of people in the world who need things more than we need to go to the beach. If he did this for us, I'd have to assume that he was doing it for everybody else all over the world. So this sort of fluxing and fading in and out of existence, this mutation would almost have to be the constant state of the world.

Well . . . either it was all magic, unreliable and intangible, or it was all real and solid, and it worked the way it always seemed to work. Kenny and Percella were either fifty miles away or they weren't. They were either almost here and we'd go to the beach, or they weren't and we might not. I dropped it. I didn't mention this to David or Philip; I just hoped we'd get to go to the beach.

As it turned out, they didn't show up for another hour.

Later, when I got into witchcraft and Satanism, it wasn't much of a leap. Magic is magic, after all. It didn't matter who your God was, what colors he wore, what gang he ran. What mattered, ultimately, was how much of a hassle he was. Satan wasn't much of a hassle; he offered just as much free magical assistance as the other guy, and he came through just as often—about 50 percent of the time, I supposed. About the same odds as pure chance.

At least Satan didn't pretend to give a shit about innocent people and then not come through when they were pleading for him to save their lives.

— — —

Preachers were always circulating through the jail. A couple of weeks later another one came in, looking pretty much just like the other ones: pasty, dead-eyed, and poorly dressed. This one was hard to get rid of. He started out all right enough, asked me some general questions about why I thought I was there. Then he began to try to convert me aggressively.

"Robbery, man. I know why I'm here."

"But don't you think maybe there's another reason?"

"No. I robbed somebody. That's pretty much enough."

"Maybe it's because God wasn't in your life."

"I doubt it," I said. I didn't feel like talking. I'd let him in only to be nice. "Look," I said, "I think I'm gonna take a nap."

"Well, let me read you something," he said, and opened his Bible.

"No, that's all right."

He started reading anyway.

"Look," I said, "I told you I wanted to take a nap, all right?"

The preacher got up, huffed, and knocked on my cell door for a guard to let him out.

When he left I said, "Take it easy." He didn't respond.

— — —

I never let them in my cell after that. What a sad game it all was. They swarm us in jail, at literally the lowest point of our lives, and try to exploit that misery to make converts. The convict has zero power, and is scared to death. If he can befriend anybody who might be in a position to help him, he will.

But these preachers couldn't help anybody. It gave them something to do, and it gave them a sense of power. They had no real power, of course. They were about the least effective people I'd ever seen. Look at Arnold, the most convincing born-again around. He'd swallowed a whole world of Jesus, and now that he was up with the apes, he was just like the rest of them, and Jesus was nowhere around.

[TWENTY-TWO]

The train tracks ran from the farmhouse into Brickville, right past my house—it was a two-mile hike, a passage that I often used when I skipped school or ran away from home. I was walking the tracks where there weren't any tracks anymore, even the wooden ties had disappeared, just an elevated line of giant pieces of gravel that passed by my house and continued alongside a little creek with no name, straight past the park and baseball diamonds and basketball courts where the old ominous four-story nineteenth-century redbrick school building used to stand, out on the north end of town, and out into the woods and through and above cornfields and soybean fields, right over the creek by the farmhouse on the old iron trestle, a skeleton of a structure with gaps in the iron girders that looked down twenty feet to the water.

It was a hot midsummer day; I was fourteen years old, almost fifteen, and I walked past the ball diamonds.

The place was packed with people. There were games going on, kids running around, adults drinking beer and yelling shit at their children on the field. "Get the fucking ball, you little cocksucker, before I take you home and beat your ass!"

I was wearing a dark green knee-length WWII army overcoat with the shoulder insignia of an artillery man, a baseball-style camouflage military cap with the visor pulled down just over my eyes. My hands were in my pockets and I was holding the coat closed. Each hand, concealed in the deep pockets, clutched the grip of a pistol—in my left was a .25 automatic with a six-shot clip and in my right was a .380 automatic with a seven-shot clip. If I were to let my coat fall open, two .22 revolvers, one black and the other gold, would be visible stuffed into my waistband, no doubt a bit shocking to all those barbarian dipshits I was walking past.

Additional firepower and killing devices: a .32 derringer in my left boot and a .410 shotgun slung by a leather strap over my right shoulder, also concealed under the long, heavy coat. I suppose if someone looked closely, they would have been able to see the barrel poking down beneath the hem of my coat. On my belt were pouches full of extra ammunition and two large hunting knives, one serrated and one not, their blades seven or eight inches long. All the weapons except for the serrated knife and the shotgun belonged to my father.

I walked quickly though the park, getting a few looks and one or two pointing fingers. One redneck even yelled, "Hey, boy, you going to war?" and all his cohorts laughed like fucking buffoons. I considered right then just dropping the coat and filling them all with holes, but I kept walking, without looking back.

That was the first time I ran away. My brother showed up at the farmhouse on his motorcycle two hours after I got there and found Philip and me shooting at cans in the creek. He had discovered my escape, had checked my father's gun collection and come out to retrieve me. He took me home and I put the guns away—he didn't try to shame me, didn't really say much at all, but just looked very serious and disturbed. I don't think he had any idea at all what to say to me.

— — —

I started wearing my hair longer, bangs down over my eyes, with pocket T-shirts and jeans, and I started slouching. I smoked in the woods by the school with Rich Bass and Charlie Bender—Charlie had become a badass, a real badass nobody fucked with.

Rich said, "Shit, Nate, you smoke?"

"Fuck yeah, I smoke." I didn't inhale, though.

Charlie said, "You're all right, man."

And from then on . . . I went with it. Knocked people out when they stood too close or looked at me wrong. I put blood on the hallways, made jokes that weren't really jokes about burning down the school, about killing the teachers, about machine-gunning kids. I said Satan was my master, Satan wanted me to kill . . . and they all backed way the hell off.

This was an epiphany. It came like a revelation.

I said to Philip one day, "You can't be a part of the in-crowd because you can't afford the clothes. As it stands you can't make fucking jokes in class because those cunts make fun of you. It's like you're not allowed to participate in society. They got a lock on it all. You can't play their game because they've got it rigged. Well, fuck them and their fucking game. Stay on the outside. Make 'em afraid. Be dangerous, right? Be *beyond* it all. It's easy. Just be willing to do whatever it takes. Be willing to be scarier than the next guy."

"Fucking A!" Philip smacked his fist into the palm of his other hand.

I started ticking off the tenets of my new lifestyle: "Satanism, anarchy, black leather, heavy metal, chains, barbarian jewelry, ripped-up jeans. Always be armed, with the brass knuckles and the blades. Steal, fight, terrorize . . . be *willing*, man—that's all it takes. Be willing to inspire fear, and fuck up anybody who gets in your way."

And that's what I did.

— — —

Few things are scarier than an apparently homicidal Satan worshipper. Philip became as infatuated with witchcraft as I was. We aspired to be, in our own words, warlocks, absolute evil with absolute power. We believed in magic, the power of spells—if the book said you had to dig up the skull of a dead five-year-old child, grind it to powder, and mix it with two parts goat milk and one part your own blood in order to see the future, we were looking for the most secluded cemetery to rob. Philip said he knew of one in Kentucky, a very old cemetery from the seventeen or eighteen hundreds on his grandparents' property, where no one would see us. We never made the trip—neither of us had a car and neither of us had money.

— — —

Philip threw down the last tarot card and said solemnly, "Nate, you are not going to die young. You'll get a job in a factory and have a miserable ugly wife and disgusting kids and you'll blow your head off with a 12-gauge when you're fifty."

I just looked at him.

"I'm serious." He threw up his hands. "It's in the fucking cards, man!"

"Fuck you. It's not in the goddamn cards. You're misinterpreting them."

"I'm not misinterpreting shit, man. Look, right there, the guy with the cups—over here, the death card . . ."

I started to gather up the cards.

"What are you doing?" he asked.

"They're my cards, man. When you know what you're fucking doing, I'll let you read them."

— — —

One time when I spent the night with Philip and David, Philip got caught stealing cigarettes from his dad and the old fucker came up to his room and knocked the piss out of him right in front of me. Philip and I conspired that night to liberate ourselves. This was our plan: We sneak out the upstairs window around three a.m., when everyone's asleep, climb down the side of the house on a metal structure that was used to support a huge television antenna, walk the tracks all the way to Shoshone, a town even smaller than Brickville, about ten miles away. There we'd get a friend to drive us to Lake Town in the north of the state, where a guy I had met through some friends in another small town a couple of miles from Brickville lived. This guy was in with the Lake Town chapter of a major gang (of which he was probably the only local member—but we imagined it to be a whole secret army). We'd join up and either sell enough drugs or get involved in enough capers to finance a trip to California, where we'd join the Church of Satan.

That night we walked ten miles in six inches of snow, freezing the whole way. There was a full moon, and with all the light reflecting off the snow, it was clear as day and dead silent. We trudged on and discussed our plans. Philip was ecstatic. He hugged me numerous times, told me he loved me. About three hours into the hike, it began to snow again, but by now we were well past Brickville and only an hour or so from our destination. We hid out for a while in an old barn, afraid that if we fell asleep, we'd freeze to death.

It was too early to knock on anybody's door. The kid still lived with his parents, and parents generally regard with suspicion two hoods who show up at their door in the wee hours of the morning.

"We could build a fire," Philip said.

"Somebody might see us. Call the cops."

"Yeah."

"Just think of California, man. Sunshine. Hot-ass girls."

"I'm still cold." He shivered.

"Me too."

We put it off for as long as we could, but when we got too cold, too exhausted, and too hungry, we had to bite the bullet. We had to get inside. After tapping at the kid's bedroom window for about fifteen minutes, unable to wake him, we finally went to the front door and rang the bell. When his mother answered the door in her nightgown and robe, we made up a story about my mom dropping us off on her way to work. Our friend, who had been sleeping soundly in a warm bed all night, the only friend we had who owned a vehicle, our only chance at escape, came to the door with sleepy eyes.

"What are you guys doing?" he asked.

I said, "We're going to California, man."

"To join the Church of Satan," Philip added.

"Are you nuts?"

"No," I said. "We need you to drive us to Lake Town."

"You *are* nuts."

"Come on, man." I punched him in the shoulder. "What else have you got to do today?"

"Not go to Lake Town," he said. "I'll give you a ride home, but that's it."

While he got dressed, Philip and I waited by the door.

"This is bullshit," Philip said.

"I know."

In the truck, I said, "Man, it's only, what, two hours away?"

Then, rather emphatically, our friend said, "I'm taking you home. *I am not driving to Lake Town.*"

"Okay," I said. "Don't get pissed."

"Yeah, Jesus," Philip said. "It's no big deal. Let's go home."

[TWENTY-THREE]

In P-14, the cell next to mine, was a young wiry black guy named Timmon. I don't know what he was in for, maybe assault and battery—no, probably burglary; he was too much of a pussy for assault and battery. He was loud and a moron and he needed the radio on twenty-four hours a day.

There were little speakers in the corridors outside our cells through which the guards would pipe music. Generally it was from a classic rock radio station, but sometimes it was country. It all depended who was in Control that day. Control was a room behind mirrored glass down by Sallyport where they have a panel of video monitors to observe all the parts of the jail. Every corridor and every cell block had a camera in it. Control controlled everything, even the radio station.

The guards would turn the speakers on and off if you

asked them. Timmon liked to eat with the radio on, shit with it on, even sleep with it on. I'd ask a guard to turn the damn thing off and immediately Timmon would be banging on his fucking door screaming like a retard because he couldn't stand the silence. There was no peace. At first Timmon and I got along. He even traded me a cigarette for some magazines one time—the first cigarette I'd had in six months. But those were the good old days—back when Timmon wasn't driving me nuts with that fucking radio.

One day, Josh walked by and I said, "Dude, will you please turn that speaker off? I can't stand it." So he did.

Timmon went crazy, started kicking his door.

I looked at Josh and said, "Walk away, man. Please, just walk away." So he did.

Timmon yelled to me, "I'll kick your fucking ass, you little motherfucker."

I yelled back, "Listen up, cocksucker. I'll gut you like a fucking groundhog if you don't shut the fuck up!"

"What?" he said. "You'll gut me like a *groundhog*? What are you, some kind of backwoods redneck? Fuck you, cracker! I want the radio back!" And he started kicking his door again.

I yelled, "Timmon, sit down and shut up!"

"Fuck you, cracker!"

So because this was the *second* time he called me a cracker, which is a racial slur in itself, I felt it only appropriate to respond with, "All right, nigger, I'm cutting your motherfucking throat."

"Whoa!" Timmon yelled, out of his mind now. "You call me a *nigger*, white boy? You think you can call me a nigger and live?"

"How many times do you expect to call me a cracker and not be called a nigger? Think about it, retard."

"That's it. When these doors open, I'm coming in there. It's *on*, motherfucker."

"Okay," I said. "It's on, then."

Then, miraculously, Timmon quieted down, and I went to sleep.

Later that evening I was awakened by Leonard at my door. He was pushing a mop bucket. "You wanna clean your cell, Henry?"

"No," I said.

"You sure?"

"Yeah." I just wanted to sleep. Then I heard Timmon in the hallway.

"Fuck no, he don't want you to open that door. He knows I'll kick his fucking ass."

Shit. I had forgotten. So I got up and pulled my sweatpants on. Leonard opened the door and I went out, stood a few feet in front of Timmon, who was several inches taller than me. I threw my hands up and said, "Okay, let's go."

There was a tense moment when I waited for him to strike, but then he broke out into laughter and said, "Shit, boy, you're fucking crazy," and went to mopping his own cell.

So I went back into my cell, Leonard closed and locked the door behind me, and I went back to sleep. That was the closest I ever came to actually being in a fight in jail, and I suppose it wasn't much. Timmon was at least a bit less obsessed with the radio after that. Which was nice, finally.

I thought a lot about the Timmon incident afterward. I knew that when I went to prison, they weren't going to back down. I hadn't expected Timmon to back down. I didn't *want* to fight him. I didn't want it on my record, but I had to take the challenge. I'd seen enough prison movies to know that you never, under any circumstances, back down from a fight. Never show any weakness. I had been weak with Arnold. Having backed down from Arnold in the beginning, allowing him to torment me with the whistling—it bothered me. It made me doubt myself.

I was trying to prepare myself for prison. I was trying to get myself sharp. I didn't know how to do that, other than to accept that everything was expendable, especially physical health. This is hard to do. It's terrifying. I was a scrawny kid, a hundred and thirty pounds, five foot seven. I didn't have any tattoos at the time. I looked like a boy. Compared to most of those apes I saw in the rec yard, I knew I was a victim waiting to happen, fresh meat. So I had decided that when I went to prison, I would carry a finely sharpened pencil with me at all times, and the first big cocksucker who got in front of me was getting stabbed in the throat. That was the only way

I could see to establish any kind of threatening presence. This of course meant a murder rap on top of the robbery rap and possibly life in prison. But life in prison with the reputation of a killer might be a whole lot better than fourteen years of torture.

[TWENTY-FOUR]

I remember standing in my brother's room, leaning against his door while he fiddled with something, perhaps worked on the final stages of building a sword—he was always making swords and daggers and billy clubs, and we'd often sword fight in the alley beside our house—and as I was standing there watching him do this, I tried to express to him my great fascination with crime. Thanks to my dad, I had always had a steady dose in the form of movies about gangsters and thieves of all kinds.

I said, "Man, I want to be like Al Capone. I want to be like Dillinger, man, wanted by the FBI and on the run. I want a rap sheet a foot thick: public enemy number one."

My brother nodded and occasionally looked up and said something only minutely discouraging, but really he was just listening.

"What about prison?" he finally asked.

"They all went to prison at some point, or were killed. That's just part of the game." I shrugged. "Do some time if you have to. No big deal. But to have *done* all of those things! That's the point."

And indeed that *was* the point. To have done. I was more interested in having an interesting history than in carrying out the acts themselves.

This had been true with my fascination with all things military as well. When I was forming the Black Hawks, I had visions of becoming a fascist leader, of clawing my way to the top by ruthless means. I desperately wanted to be a Hitler or a Stalin, and if that wasn't possible, then I wanted to be a leader of organized crime. I saw myself at rallies moving tens of thousands to rapture by the passion of my speech.

Philip and I would engage in small-time criminal acts, like breaking into abandoned houses or stealing cigarettes from the carryout next door to my house. One night he and David and I, decked out in our mercenary uniforms, black face paint and all, made our way into town. We slashed the tires on a car owned by a guy who owed money to a guy David knew, and we busted out the windows in the mayor's garage. We were chased through the streets by somebody who happened to drive by and see us—he didn't see us slash the tires or bust the windows, but he saw us crouching beside someone's trailer afterward regaining our breath. We split up and ran in different directions.

I was the one he caught up to. Completely out of

breath after a ten-minute sprint, I gasped and heaved in the shadows behind a church. He pulled his car directly in front of me, said, "What's going on?"

"Nothing." I was still out of breath.

"What were you guys doing back there?"

"Halloween prank," I said. I considered bashing the guy in the face and running, but I was too weak.

He looked at me for a long moment, apparently realizing there wasn't much he could do.

"Okay, I'll tell them." He drove away. Tell who? Maybe the people who lived in the trailer we were crouching beside. I don't know.

I was bleeding. I had used the handle of a knife to shatter those windows, and a shard of glass had penetrated my leather half-gloves and sliced my right middle finger down to the bone. When David and Philip and I finally met up at our rendezvous, I peeled the glove off while David shined a flashlight and saw that my hand was covered with blood. I felt weak. There was so much blood, and it continued to drip from my fingers at such a rate that I was afraid I was going to bleed to death.

The trip back to the farmhouse was long and slow, but I made it, and managed to stop the bleeding with gauze and a bandage.

— — —

And we stole a lot. I spent a great deal of time hanging around the carryout beside our house. I knew the woman who worked there and she liked me, so I'm sure that she was quite torn when she discovered that she was missing five cartons' worth of individual packs of cigarettes after Philip and I had spent an hour there. But she never said anything. Every time she'd look away, we'd pocket two or three packs. At night, at the farmhouse, we opened the duffel bag to show our loot to David. He was amazed and thoroughly impressed. Fifty packs in an hour each. What a fucking score. Sure, they were all different brands, most of them generic, but nonetheless, even if we had to divvy them up three ways, we would be fully stocked for weeks.

Every year at school, the sophomore band members would sell candy bars to raise money for their cause, whatever the hell that was—new uniforms perhaps. So suddenly there were hundreds of boxes of candy bars floating around the school, going for a dollar each. David and I decided that we couldn't let this opportunity pass, so we began to break into the sophomores' lockers. Those lockers are normally pretty secure, but then again, I had perfected my lock-picking abilities in pursuit of my dad's porn, which he kept locked away in his den. We accumulated several boxes of candy bars and began to sell them to students at fifty cents a pop—we made a killing. But soon enough, our names got to the principal and we knew that we were about to be rounded up. David and I were no strangers to the principal's office. I was usually sent there a couple of times a week for some kind of disturbance. Later, in the next year or two, those visits would become more frequent, and I would end up there every day for one reason or another. But this time, before the gestapo came for us, we came up with a plan.

We had to unload the remaining boxes of evidence, and there were still several boxes.

There was a kid named Jeremy Sproggs who we'd always hated. Why we hated him is not entirely clear. He was not a *likable* kid—in fact he punched me once for no good reason in fifth grade, but I was not one to hold a grudge for something like that for four years. Perhaps he was just an easy mark, and since he was not well liked, he would make a decent patsy. So we broke into his locker and hid the boxes beneath some jackets.

We were sitting in the principal's office and he was trying to intimidate us, talking about calling the sheriff, threatening to charge us with theft. We could both be expelled and incarcerated, he said. My arms were crossed and my legs were kicked out and I even yawned a couple of times—I was as cool as I could be, totally unbothered. David exhibited the same gangster imperturbability. When the principal finished his spiel, he asked me, "So, where is the candy?" I said I didn't know.

"I have no idea why you suspect me of knowing," I said. "I haven't seen any stolen candy, but I have *heard* about it. Everyone's heard about it."

"You're saying you don't know *anything* about this?"

I stared at him for a few moments, pretending to deliberate. "There are *rumors*," I finally said. "I've heard a name, but I'm not sure I want to tell you the name I've heard. I'm not a rat, man."

"Well." Mr. Callander sighed. "You guys are the prime suspects right now. Everything points to you."

Now it was David's turn. "Look," he said. "I'll tell you what we know if you promise not to tell anybody that we told you. If people find out that I gave you a name . . ." And David shook his head like he didn't even want to *imagine* the consequences.

The principal put his hands together and leaned on his desk. I'm sure he wasn't taken in by this, but he was going along nonetheless. "Okay," he said. "It'll be between us."

"Okay." David pretended that moral conflict was tearing him to pieces. He swallowed hard and glanced at me. I shrugged like it was out of my hands. He then looked back at the principal. "Jeremy Sproggs," he said. "We heard that Jeremy was the one who stole the candy and that he keeps it in his locker."

So poor Jeremy, unsuspecting of his fate, probably sat in math class struggling over a problem, nothing further from his mind than the possibility of being framed for a crime he didn't commit—as far as I know he never committed any crimes, got decent grades, and aside from that punching incident in fifth grade, never caused any trouble at all. When those bastards were finished with Jeremy's locker, his things were strewn about the hall like it was the scene of a natural disaster. And there was the candy, right in the bottom of his locker. They took photographs for evidence. And that poor bastard was expelled on twenty counts of theft, one per box of candy, his high school record forever marred by a shameful act he didn't commit.

If I ever meet Jeremy again, I'll apologize to him, and hopefully he won't punch me too hard a second time.

— — —

When I was fifteen, I got hold of a book called *Say You Love Satan*. It was the true story of a teenager in New York who'd stabbed another kid to death in what looked like a ritual sacrifice. This is why the book sold so well— nice and sensational. Of course when you read the thing, you see that it doesn't look like a ritual sacrifice at all. It looks like a fucked-up kid whacked out on hallucinogens getting caught up in the moment and making a terrible mistake. Happens all the time.

It was a thick book, a few hundred pages. I read the thing over and over. I carried it everywhere. It became my bible. I modeled myself after the lead character, Ricky Kasso. I occasionally asked myself, "What would Ricky do?"

I stopped working in school. I slept or read my book in most of my classes and got suspended whenever I could. If the kids at school weren't afraid of me before, this Satanism kick really pushed it across the line. I was in the principal's office every other day. I had completely given up. Graduating was no longer a possibility, but my parents would never agree to let me drop out, so my plan was simply to wait it out. As soon as I was eighteen, I'd leave school, hitchhike to LA, and live on the streets. There's a Guns N' Roses song called "Nightrain" that sums up what I wanted to do perfectly. The lyrics are all about getting fucked up and staying fucked up. That was all I wanted to do for the rest of my life. I always imagined I'd be screwing some bimbo who had a job, and she'd pay for everything. I imagined getting up late in the afternoon, taking some speed to get going, drinking and doing coke all night, and then taking some downers to sleep, waking up twelve hours later with some speed, and the cycle continues.

At my last parent-teacher conference, Mr. Simpson, my history teacher, asked me what I thought I'd be doing in five years. I said, "Living on the streets in LA."

My mom hit me in the arm and said, "Seriously."

I said, "Okay, seriously. I imagine myself as a janitor in a fast-food restaurant."

She just shook her head, very disappointed.

[TWENTY-FIVE]

Kline came by and kicked my cell door. He said, "We just got another juvie in."

I went to the door and leaned against the jamb. "Oh, yeah? What'd he do?"

Kline shook his head. "He's charged with murder."

"Holy fuck," I said. "Who'd he kill?"

Kline said, "I didn't say he *killed* anybody, I said he was *charged* with murder."

"All right," I said, "then who is he *charged* with murdering?"

Kline shook his head and made a snarl of disgust. "An old lady," he said. "In her own home. Strangled to death. You want him for a cellmate?"

"I don't know, man. Let me think about it."

"All right, you'll meet him tomorrow; you'll go to rec together. Just let us know."

Then he kicked my door again and walked away.

I sat back down on my bunk to mull it over. A killer. An old-lady killer. Wow, I thought. A real murderer. I thought a lot about it that night, but I didn't know *what* to think about it. The variables were numerous. I imagined a hard and mean kid, a criminal so tough and crude he'd make me and all my former cellmates, including Arnold, look like a bunch of pussies, a cold-blooded predator with nothing to lose. I imagined him shanking me in my sleep and fucking my dead body.

But the next day, when it came time for rec, Josh came by and unlocked my door and there the killer was, standing in the hallway, a well-groomed white kid with freshly scrubbed skin and not a hint of facial hair. He looked like he hadn't yet reached puberty. I nodded and he smiled back—not a malicious smile, but a rather polite smile. I walked behind Josh as we headed down the corridor toward the elevator, and this kid moved up beside me, asked me what I was in for. He asked it in a real phony old-gangster-movie kind of way, like he was imitating James Cagney, but he wasn't making a joke, just putting on a show.

"Armed robbery," I said. And just to be polite, "You?"

"Murder." When he said this there was a smirk on his face, like he knew the word carried a lot of weight, like he knew it would make him look tough, something he'd obviously never been.

We shot some hoops in the yard and I asked him about his crime. He said he was innocent. He said his buddy was the one who did it. He wasn't convincing, but he didn't exactly seem to be lying. There was just something very young and pretentious about him. I sized him up almost immediately as a pussy, whether he'd killed somebody or not.

There are subtle ways guys assert dominance and establish their status. After dealing with Arnold and Mo, and after watching the absurd monkey drama play itself out in the rec yard every day from my window in P-13, I knew a thing or two more than I used to. And I had always been pretty good at it, when I needed to be.

Subtle things. Not laughing at the other guy's little jokes. If he makes little jokes that are naturally uttered for his own amusement, that's one thing. Jokes intended to please others, that just cry out for approval, for laughter—those are an entirely different matter. It's a sign of weakness. If there's a point in a game where it's not clear whose turn it is, you take the turn. If you both come to a doorway at the same time, you go ahead and walk through first, pretend they don't exist. Occasionally ask pointed questions without a hint of real curiosity, and when they ask you questions, sometimes you answer and sometimes you don't. If you do, you do it with as few words as possible.

It's pretty easy after a few minutes to see where they stand. The old-lady killer deferred constantly, made jokes over and over again and asked all kinds of questions. He was no threat at all, just a kid, didn't even have a firm grasp on what he was facing, what was happening to him, so after rec, I told Josh I'd go ahead and bunk with him.

[TWENTY-SIX]

I caught Billy between the two sets of double doors at the entrance to the high school and threw him up against a wall. He had called me a pussy and spit at me from aboard his school bus at the end of the day before. I tried to board the bus—would've settled the matter then, but the driver shut the door on me and threatened to call the principal. Now I punched him in the face with both fists, one after the other; when he lifted his arms to shield his face, I punched him in the stomach; when he lowered his arms, I went back to work on his face. It went on like that for a couple of minutes, until he wasn't standing up anymore.

As far as I was concerned, I had become the super-hoodlum. I had it down, from the clothes to the walk to the bored and surly expression.

Nate, would you mind doing us a favor? Just for a minute or two; it won't take long. Thank you, Nate; we're very grateful. Go stand out there, right there for a minute. Look at me. Stand up straight. Just let your hands hang to your sides.

Let's have a look at you. Long hair—not too long but long enough—bangs in your eyes, hair on the back of your head down past your collar. Head cocked back defiantly—looks like you want to kick our asses, like you just don't give a damn. About half a dozen necklaces: silver chains, a choker, a giant Anarchy symbol medallion on a leather bootlace. A black leather motorcycle jacket, a black concert T-shirt.

What does your shirt say, Nate? Open up your jacket a little bit. There. Thank you. Metallica, *Ride the Lightning*. I suspected as much. Tight black jeans, a black leather wallet with three different chains connecting it to your belt. What's your belt buckle look like? I see, a bull's skull with red glass eyes. Black leather biker boots with nickel-plated rings on both sides, leather straps connecting them. What's that, Nate? Oh, yes, they're called harness boots. And I see you've applied some chains to your boots as well, and are those spurs? You have spurs on your boots? Why in the world would you need spurs on your boots, man? You haven't ridden a horse in years. They're what? I see. You could slash someone's throat open with them, if you could kick that high. And back to the jewelry—why don't you lift the sleeves of your jacket up. Let's see how many bracelets you have on. My God, man, I'm surprised you can lift your arms with all that metal around your wrists. Oh, they give your fists more weight when you have to punch someone.

Well, that makes sense. Do you have to punch people a lot? Suspended three times this year for assault. Hmm. Well, it's a mystery to me why you're still on the street with a temper like that.

What have you got in your pockets? Go ahead and empty your pockets. Don't worry; we're not going to confiscate anything. We just want to see. I'll bet anything you've got at least one kind of deadly weapon. Unbelievable. Do you realize that if a policeman searched you he could arrest you for having things like that? You don't care. Pair of brass knuckles, a leather blackjack, a switchblade knife—is that really a switchblade? You ever use it? Not yet. But you will if you have to. This town has a population of something like a thousand people, man. It's not New York or Los Angeles, where someone might actually need protection, where someone encounters danger on a daily basis. *You're* probably the only real danger that people around here ever encounter. Do you know that? And what do you think about that? What's that? Fuck them? Okay, well, thank you for your time, Nate. You can go now.

[TWENTY-SEVEN]

The old-lady killer's name was Dicky. He strangled a seventy-seven-year-old woman with a phone cord in her own home. We were cellmates for only a couple of weeks. I just couldn't take it.

Dicky was effeminate and prissy, and he would surely be raped mercilessly in prison. Dicky's life might very well end the moment he got to prison. But he was so immature, I don't think he ever worried about his future. It was all sort of a game to him, this time in jail just some extended holiday, like summer camp. He maintained his innocence about the grandma killing as long as I knew him. He said he was hiding while his friend committed the actual murder. He could have been telling the truth—I don't know.

Let me tell you a little bit about Dicky. Dicky walked like a bitch. He talked like a bitch: a somewhat high-pitched lilting voice, and if he didn't actually have a lisp, he was dangerously close to having one. His concerns were bitches' concerns.

When I first met Dicky, he had more toiletries than any inmate I ever saw. I had a toothbrush, some soap, and a towel—some shampoo too. On top of what I had, which is what every inmate had, which is what they'd give you for free if you didn't buy anything from commissary, Dicky had hairspray, deodorant, mousse, two or three different brands of toothpaste, an arsenal of brushes and combs, hand lotion, foot cream, facial cream, moisturizing body lotion—you name it, he fucking had it.

I'd been writing poetry for a while. When Dicky met me, he started writing poetry too, but his poems were shitty and emotional—if I would have described my own work as bricks and razors and whiskey bottles, I'd have described his as melted ice cream and deflated birthday balloons. I thought he was a moron. He had no balls.

I'm not saying I necessarily thought Dicky was gay, and even if I did think he was gay, that wouldn't have been the only reason he drove me nuts. It was the totality of Dicky that annoyed me. It was his preening, effeminate, undermining viciousness. It was everything.

I didn't hate gays for being gay anymore. I had hated them when I was younger—I didn't know why. I had thought they were *naturally* detestable, inherently wrong. I didn't think I needed a reason. I'd hated blacks too.

When I first got to jail, I got a book off the library cart—I can't remember what it was, one of the first books I tried to read in there. Within the first couple of pages,

I came upon a scene where a couple of guys pull over to the side of a dark country road to take a piss, and as the one guy was pissing, the other guy was watching him. The guy who was watching got a hard-on when he saw the other guy's dick. I almost vomited when I read that. I threw the book across my cell and couldn't touch it or look at it for a few days. I tossed a T-shirt over it so I wouldn't have to see it. It seemed diseased and I felt that perhaps I had contracted something from reading it. I felt that I had been violated. I feared that I'd been infected.

Since that time, I have found that I absolutely love the writers Jack Kerouac, William Burroughs, Allen Ginsberg, and Arthur Rimbaud. With the exception of Kerouac, they were all gay, and even Jack fucked around with his male friends. Hell, there is even good reason to believe Jim Morrison was bisexual.

I gave it a lot of thought and I just could not find an adequate reason to hate gays for being gay. When I thought about their gayness, I still felt a little sick, but I was trying to get over it. Feeling sick was not a good enough reason in itself.

So I was a more enlightened man when I met Dicky. And though Dicky disgusted me in a lot of ways, it was not necessarily his effeminacy that made me want, on more than one occasion, to smash his face.

He was a failure of a human being all the way to his core. Socially inept, needy, sheltered. And he was always trying to correct me when I misused a word. He was such a nag that I finally almost beat his ass one night, but just before I punched him, I glanced up and there was Josh, looking in our window. I said, "Josh, get me the fuck out of here or, so help me, I'm gonna kill this fucking faggot."

So I was back to P-13 once again.

[TWENTY-EIGHT]

I still had not been laid, and this was supremely important. It was a huge problem. How badass can you be if
you're a virgin? But I had come close.

I met Lauren at a fishing pond fifteen miles outside of
town. David, Philip, and I would camp there some weekends. It was a members-only fishing spot, so it was never
too crowded. One night we met a girl who was around
fifteen. I was fifteen too by this point, and I was desperate to find a girlfriend.

I'd tried at school to seduce girls, but my reputation
had destroyed all chance. There was an Italian girl in
particular with massive breasts. Her name was Jennifer
D'Nozzio and she had two little mean-ass brothers who
were apparently the new tough kids in school. I got along
with them all right—I mean, they'd nod at me in the
hallways. I figured if they were ever in a scrap, I'd help
out. So I asked Jennifer if she wanted to go out. She said

yes, to my total amazement, but by the end of the day she'd been warned by other people at the school that I was a pariah, and I was accosted by her two brothers in the hallway. They thought they were mafia.

"Scumbag, leave my sister alone," one of them said, as he stuck a finger in my chest.

"Fuck you." I knocked his hand aside.

Both brothers moved in closer, just like real thugs, real hired muscle, and I realized that I'd never be able to kick both their asses.

"What'd you say?" one of them said.

I considered fighting them, even though I'd surely end up smeared on the floor, but at least I'd have taken a stand. But the principle of it demoralized me. Jennifer obviously didn't want me, and I just felt sad.

"Fine." I turned around and walked away.

Back to the pond. Lauren was a crazy girl from Plantation, seemed up for anything. Philip told her out of the blue, for no real apparent reason, "Yeah, Nate's gonna bend you over good!"

She replied, "Cool, I'd let him if my dad wasn't here."

I couldn't believe my ears. I was going to get laid after all! So I made a date with her for the next weekend. My mom's family still lived in Plantation and she visited all the time. I'd go with her next week and meet up with Lauren.

Everything went as planned, sort of, and I met up with her. All we did was walk around. I had no idea what to do. I'm sure she really was up for anything, but I was at a total loss. We just sort of walked around and that was it—we didn't even hold hands. I didn't try to kiss her until I was leaving, and then all I did was peck her on the cheek.

We talked on the phone after that, and it turned out that she had an extra ticket for the Guns N' Roses and Skid Row show that was coming up in a week. It just so happened that these were my two absolute favorite bands in the world and I would've done anything to see them live. Lauren offered me the ticket, and my mom actually said I could go and then spend the night at Lauren's house. I couldn't imagine anything better. See Guns N' Roses and Skid Row and definitely get laid. I would never have dreamed such things were possible. But when the night of the concert finally came, I couldn't get ahold of her. I called a dozen times and waited all night to hear from her, but she didn't call.

She didn't call all that week. By the time the weekend rolled around, I went to Plantation with my mom and walked to her house, decked out in a jean jacket with the sleeves cut off and a bandanna on my head. I knocked on her door. Her mom answered and sent me upstairs to Lauren's room. She didn't seem surprised to see me. She was practically naked, in panties and a bra, standing in front of her mirror brushing her wet hair. I sat on her bed and chain-smoked.

"You go to that concert?" I asked.

She looked at my reflection in the mirror and said, "It was fucking awesome."

I looked at her breasts. I looked at her panties. I should've been horny as fuck, but I felt nauseous. I'd been chain-smoking, and the way she so casually fucked me out of the greatest night of my life got to me in a bad way.

"Awesome, huh?"

She nodded.

I had a Pepsi can in my hand that I'd been using for an ashtray. The nausea got worse, and I knew I was going to vomit. Then it happened. I tried to direct the puke into the Pepsi can, but some of it splashed out around the can and onto the floor. I got to my feet and wiped my mouth.

She turned around from the mirror, looking disgusted.

"God!" she said.

I dropped the can on the floor.

"I don't want to see you again," I said.

As I ran down the stairs I could hear her respond with: "That's all right with me, psycho!"

[TWENTY-NINE]

Josh came by my door and asked me if I wanted to go to rec. It was raining, so it would be inside. I wondered if Dicky the Grandma Slayer would be there. He hadn't been around yesterday. I thought, "Maybe somebody finally shanked his ass. If he's around, we'll play Ping-Pong, and if he isn't, I guess I'll look out the window and watch the street." It's about the only room in the building from which you can see a street that's very busy at all.

Josh said he'd be back in a minute. There might have been a fight down in C-18, the cell block at the end of the hall. I'd heard a bunch of noise earlier from that direction, around six thirty, and several of the guards had run past my door. That's where Josh was headed. He was pushing the mop bucket, had rubber gloves on—probably going to clean up some blood. Where the hell were the trustees? They normally did that kind of nasty shit.

Josh was a nice guy, but I always had the impression that the other guards took a shit on him. He wasn't cut out for high-stress work. He got this look on his face when he was pushed too far, like he was going to snap emotionally and he didn't know what to do with himself. I never thought he was capable of being violent, though. I thought he would throw something or kick something, like a desk or a door.

He had a Harley apparently, a Heritage Classic—big fucking bike. He showed me a picture of it. Black with a lot of chrome. If he ever went to biker rallies, the other bikers probably picked on him, made him buy their beer, and he'd probably go off to get their beer with that same irate spastic look on his face he got in the jail when things got too stressful. But who knows? Maybe I was wrong. Maybe Josh *was* a hard-ass after all. Maybe that look was the look he got when he tried to control his violent temper, and if he ever let the dark side take over, there'd be bodies all over the place.

He finally came back and took me to the rec room.

Dicky didn't come down, so I watched the street and hoped girls with nice asses would walk by so at night I could try to remember what they looked like while I jerked off. But, like I said, it was raining, so no hot girls walked by. Nobody walked by.

I hated to admit it, but I felt a little lonely without Dicky. At least we could have played some Ping-Pong.

[THIRTY]

In Brickville, Charlie Bender was king of the hoods. I idolized the kid, not just because he had a reputation as the baddest dude around, but because he was a genuinely respectable human being. He could carry on conversations with adults, and seemed perfectly comfortable, in charge of himself, reasonable. The adults would nod while he talked, and consider what he said. Charlie wore a leather motorcycle jacket and a denim sleeveless jacket over top of that. He had straight black hair down to his ass. He was only five feet two inches tall, but he commanded the world. He walked with his head held high and no one ever challenged his authority.

I had two groups of friends by the time I was fifteen. I had David and Philip, who lived out on the farm, and then there was the gang of hoods in Brickville. When I decided that I wanted to join their hierarchy, I started out by lingering around the edge of the group and slowly worked my way to Charlie's side. This was a kind of social climbing for me. Charlie was at the top, and I couldn't settle for being a hanger-on. I had to be tight with the guy at the top—or *be* the guy at the top—or I wouldn't be a part of it at all.

I sat beside Charlie in math class, back before he got kicked out. The math teacher was a timid Christian woman who, after she saw me reading the Satanic bible in class, began wearing a giant crucifix around her neck. With almost no provocation one day, Charlie challenged her.

"Why do you keep kicking us around?" he said. As far as I had seen, she hadn't kicked anyone around, but if Charlie felt like harassing a teacher, more power to him.

"What are you talking about?" she asked.

"What, just because we're poor, you think you can treat us like scum?"

"I've never treated you like scum."

"You think just because I'm poor, and because I dress like this, I must be on drugs, right?"

"No, I don't."

"Well, go ahead and ask me. Ask me if I'm on drugs."

She looked at him with a faint smile.

"Come on, ask me."

"Are you on drugs?"

"Fuck yeah, I'm on drugs. I'm always on drugs."

Charlie was eventually kicked out of school for throwing a chair at another teacher. He had also been locked up for a while. We'd all seen him fight. He was fast and mean. All it took to make a rep for yourself was audacious action like kicking the hell out of someone in front of the whole school, or telling a teacher to go fuck themselves, and I was becoming pretty good at both of those. In no time I was regarded by almost all the kids in the school as a vicious fighter, the kind of guy who was likely to do anything. Other guys might sneak cigarettes between classes, talk a lot of trash about how they were going to beat somebody's ass, but when *I* said I was going to beat somebody's ass, I did it, right in front of everybody. I stood out. While the teacher gave a lecture, I wandered around the classroom, passed notes blatantly, walked out of the room without permission, went outside for smoke breaks.

The headquarters for the hoods was the pizza shop, which was right in the center of town, right on the only intersection with a stoplight. There were tables and chairs up front, some video games, and a back room with a pool table. At any given time you could find eight or nine hoods hanging around the place.

Because my parents wouldn't let me hang out openly at the pizza shop, I'd have to make surreptitious appearances. I'd tell Mom and Dad I was going up to the post office to check the mail and I'd stop in for a smoke, chat a minute with the guys, and then head back home. This was really all that was necessary.

— — —

I was walking down an alley with Charlie Bender. It was on one of the days that I skipped school. I skipped all the time. I'd leave the house in the morning, call the school from a pay phone, and tell the secretary, "Hello, this is Mr. Henry. Nathan won't be at school today because he doesn't feel well."

"Okay," the secretary would say. "Just have him bring a note."

It worked every time, but I never took a note. One day my parents got a letter in the mail stating that I'd be failing that year because I had missed thirty-five days. They knew about two.

I'd hang up the pay phone and walk down to Charlie's house. His mom would let me in and I'd lay down on the floor of Charlie's room, pull a blanket on me, and go back to sleep.

I told Charlie, "I hate this town, man. I'm about ready to leave for good. Do some crazy shit."

"Like what?" He took a pack of Marlboro Reds out of his vest pocket, shook one out and lit it.

"I don't know." We kept walking. "Kill some motherfuckers, rob some places, go on a fucking rampage."

He shook his head. "Why would you want to do that?"

"I don't know." I was ashamed suddenly, shamed by Charlie Bender.

"You keep fucking around and you're going to end up like me, or worse. Kicked out of school. I've been to JDC too many times to count. And it ain't no fucking fun."

"I can't *wait* until I get kicked out of school."

"I ain't got nothing, man. I ain't got shit." He took a long drag off his cigarette and looked sad.

"Dude," I said. "You've made a *mark* on that place."

"What *mark*? Nobody's gonna remember me next year. It doesn't matter."

"It *always* matters," I said. "Fucking up the system always matters."

"But you're not an idiot, Nate. You can do anything you want. You can fuck with the system in ways that don't ruin you."

I stopped and lit a smoke. I laughed. "Are you counseling me?"

He looked around and got a mischievous look in his eye. "All right. Whatever. Let's go find somebody to kick the shit out of."

[THIRTY-ONE]

The coldest cell in the jail was on the third floor, just outside cell block eighteen. P-21 had no windows, so I never knew whether it was day or night, and my sleep cycles were completely out of whack. The assholes from the cell block would kick my door when they walked by sometimes, jolting me out of sleep. It was the perfect environment for a psychological breakthrough or breakdown, both of which I had, sort of, after about three weeks in that hole.

I wasn't moved from P-13 to P-21 arbitrarily. I asked for it. P-21 was just outside the mental health and substance abuse block, where the craziest born-again suckasses in the whole jail were housed. They were a meek and sinister bunch. I don't know why I thought it'd be a good idea to try to get into that area. I thought maybe it'd make the last few months of my stay easier, but it was actually an awful idea.

Adela, a petite and seemingly compassionate female guard, ran the block. She supervised the group therapy sessions and the AA meetings. It was a normal cell block in most regards except it had been painted more like a rehab center, with rainbows and, under them, stick figures with their joyous hands in the air, and posters urging the inmates that only the sky is the limit, etc. I asked Adela one day if I might be allowed to join the block, since it was obviously not full of murderous ass-rapists, and she said it was a possibility if my parents thought it was all right. Strange, but reasonable, I guess. Even though I was charged as an adult, would face trial as an adult, and was housed in an adult jail, they were still reluctant to stick me in with adults. I talked to Mom and Dad and they thought it was a decent enough idea, so Adela set up a meeting for me to introduce myself to the group. This is when they moved me to P-21. Maybe to see how I interacted with the weasels through the little window in my cell door before I actually faced them.

I moved into the dungeon with no window. Every time the group would leave for rec or come back from rec, I'd stand up by the door and nod at them, see if any of them seemed reasonable. They hated me. There was one guy in particular, a squinting psychopath who'd stare at me with his arms folded, and no matter what I said to him, like "What's up?" or "How's it going?" I got no response. Just a sneer. By the time I went into their cell block with Adela for the actual meeting, I already hated this gang of wackos. But they had a TV, a pretty snazzy cell block, and a phone they could use all the time, so I wanted to give it a shot.

Everyone sat in a circle and stared at me.

Adela said, "How could you benefit from being in the group?"

I said, "Well, it just looks like a pretty helpful environment."

"You know," she said, "everyone here is totally committed to getting through whatever problems they have. *Totally committed.* Are you?"

"Oh, yeah. Definitely."

She squinted at me. "I want to see how committed you are. Earl, will you hand Nate our charter?"

Earl, a mildly retarded-looking older guy with glasses and gray hair, got up and handed me a sheet of laminated paper. I looked at it. The first line was something about allowing our spirits to flow with charity and love. This is ridiculous, I thought.

"This is good stuff," I said.

Then she said, "Would you stand up and sing it for us?"

"What?" I asked.

"Would you stand up and sing it for us?"

"Uh." I stood up. "You want me to *sing* it for you?"

"Yeah," she said. "Just sing it."

So I sung the first line. It was not musical. My voice was shaking. It was ugly.

"Now," she said, "would you dance while you sing it to us?"

"*What*? You want me to *dance* while I *sing* this to you?"

Everyone stared at me. Adela squinted. So I sort of shuffled my feet a little and sort of sung the thing. I was humiliated. I sat back down. I wanted to kill all those fuckers, especially Adela.

"That wasn't very enthusiastic," she said. "Earl, why don't you show Nate what I mean."

Earl reached over and grabbed the sheet out of my hand with insane enthusiasm, danced up a storm, and belted those words out like he was some kind of crazed hermaphroditic diva. I was horrified. I looked from him to Adela, who had an expression on her face that was hard to pin down. It was a sort of smug satisfaction. No—it was *power*. It was *pleasure*. I hated her.

There were a couple more questions that I barely answered before I was sent back to my cell. I sat on my bunk, confused and disgusted. I didn't ever want to see any of those people again. I expected to then be transferred back to P-13, back home, back to where things were as they should be. But I wasn't. They left me there, in that little cell with no window, with those weirdos glaring in at me every time they came and went. Adela eventually told me the group decided I was not committed enough. No, I wasn't committed—I didn't know what Adela had expected from me. What were the weirdos committed to? What was Earl all about—with his nutless little song and dance? Maybe they were just scared, scared of doing more time, scared of being thrown into a real cell block. Or maybe they weren't scared at all. Maybe they were just playing along, giving Adela a constant load of shit for extra privileges, Adela licking it all up for her own reasons. It was a transaction. This struck me as maybe a key to people, to relationships. I thought about it for a long time.

The world is full of fearful people, so they bullshit each other, they lie their asses off, and even though neither person in the transaction believes a word of what the other one says, they assume the other one believes at least some of what they are saying—and in that, they feel they have achieved some bit of power. Thanks to Adela and her sick little setup, this was what the world suddenly looked like to me—not all of it, and maybe not where it counted, but bullshit, fear, and the pursuit of power did a pretty damn good job of summing up a whole lot of human relationships.

[THIRTY-TWO]

Twin brothers, Irish, reddish brown hair, pale, and kind of on the skinny side, but tough as hell. You might not think it when you looked at them, but they were hard guys. Norton and Justin O'Reilly. They lived out in the country a few miles from the Turner farm, and in the early days we'd see them every once in a while, then less later on. We never hung out with them.

Maybe a mile from the farmhouse was a spot where the creek widened a bit and became about six feet deep, which David called the fishing hole. One day, when I was thirteen or fourteen, the O'Reillys were there and tried to start a fight with us—this was before I'd ever been in a fight, so I was intimidated, and so was David. Philip, at that age, was too small to be of any use. It was David and me against the O'Reillys. And they were tougher—they were higher-quality specimens—there was no denying it. I was in track with them in middle school. We'd run the same races. Justin would come in first, Norton second, and me third, every time. We didn't fight that day at the fishing hole, but the time would come.

Norton and Justin, although twins, had opposite temperaments. Justin was a fairly smooth, calm, respectful guy, but he was tougher than Norton. The fights or near-fights were always instigated by Norton, and out of a sense of obligation, Justin would back him up. But Justin never started fights. Norton was an asshole, a loud-mouthed cocksucker who needed someday to be put in his place. He and I were in the same math class in ninth grade, and I had had enough of his shit. I called him on it one day. He was picking on a smaller kid named Billy, poking him in the chest, just generally terrorizing him. I didn't care much for Billy—in fact I myself would kick the hell out of him the next year—but for the moment, I couldn't overlook any more of what I saw as dirty mick injustice.

I said, "Norton, sit the fuck back down or I'll make you sit down."

He stared at me like he couldn't believe his ears.

"That's right," I said. "I'll knock your fucking head off, man. Leave him alone."

Norton flew into a rage. His face turned red; his nostrils flared. When he had recovered from his surge of primitive emotion, he said, "All right. Saturday. Brickville. You and me."

"All right, bitch." I smirked. "I'll see you there."

I trained for a week. In the attic of our house, I had a small gym, weight bench, and punching bag—an army duffel bag suspended from a rafter and stuffed with blankets. I still had never been in a fight, but it couldn't be that big of a deal. You approach. You punch. You punch him in the face. You keep punching until he's down on the ground, bleeding and crying. You've won. So I practiced punching. I threw thousands of punches into the duffel bag. By the time Saturday arrived, I was ready to go. I was a killing machine.

Philip had spent the night, and around noon he and I walked to the prearranged site, behind Wentler's Pond. We crossed the Black Pipe, climbed a small hill, and rounded the pond. It was behind a small factory, Wentler's Machine Shop. I'd spent my childhood playing back there. Closer to the factory you can find skids loaded down with small, strangely shaped pieces of steel. These pieces were such odd objects that they were endlessly appealing, though completely useless to me.

There they were. Norton O'Reilly and one other boy I didn't know.

"You ready to die, motherfucker?" Norton said.

I smiled. I walked straight up to him and prepared to throw my first punch. He immediately went into a frenzy, a flurry of light punches rained on me. There were several opportunities for me to nail him, but I didn't take them. I just couldn't punch him. I didn't know what to make of it. I felt such a tremendous resistance to punching another human being that I just allowed him to hammer me. Eventually, he landed one in my eye, blinding me. I felt unbelievable pain as I clutched my eye and bent over, yelling, "I can't see! I can't see!"

Norton stopped punching. The fight was over. He had won. I had lost. I was beaten, whupped, made a bitch.

— — —

Two years later, after I'd been in several more fights and had successfully beaten the shit out of at least four other boys, I found David in the lunch line at school. Standing in front of him, facing him, poking him in the chest, was Norton O'Reilly.

"What you gonna do about it? What the fuck you gonna do about it?" He kept poking David, and it was obvious that David wasn't going to do a damn thing.

Well, now I was older and more experienced. Now I was in a position to take him down. I had become a scrapper, a badass with a handful of bloody victories under my belt. The time had come, so I seized the opportunity.

I rushed up to Norton and shoved him as hard as I could. He fell back against the wall, and just as I was about to throw the first punch—my fist was raised—he yelled, "Wait!"

I paused. I shouldn't have. I immediately regretted it.

He said, "You piece of shit. I'm not getting suspended because of you."

"Fuck you, mick," I said. "I don't give a shit about suspension."

"That's because you're a fucking loser," he said. "Meet me in town, and I'll give you an ass-beating you'll never fucking forget."

I stuck a finger in his face and said, "We'll see, motherfucker." And I walked away.

Half an hour later, I was standing outside the school in a spot between two walls where I could smoke without being seen, and David was telling me that I'd made a mistake. "You can't fight Justin!" he said. "Why would you fight Justin?"

"What?" I asked. "Justin? That wasn't Norton?"

"No, man. That was Justin."

"Justin?" And I knew he was right. I felt a subtle turn in my stomach. Those fucking mick twins . . . Shit.

Justin was the tougher, the quicker, and the smarter of the two. I had never had a beef with Justin—I respected him—and I might even say that if Justin was intimidating David, then perhaps he had a good reason. Norton was the one I wanted. Redemption was what I was after, not a brand-new war.

"Fuck," I said. "I gotta go talk to him." I dropped the cigarette and ground it into the pavement, picked up the butt and stuffed it into my pocket, and went back into the school. I found Justin at his locker.

"Justin." He looked at me. "Look, man, I thought you were Norton. I really have no interest in fighting you, man. Let's just forget about it."

"I'm not forgetting anything. You started this. We're gonna fucking finish it."

This infuriated me. "All right, motherfucker. That's fine." And I walked away.

— — —

I was with David when I got off the bus. I expected Justin to be waiting at my bus stop, but he wasn't. I knew where he got off the bus, so I took off in that direction. I took my leather jacket off and gave it to David.

"Hold this," I said, which he did, for a few minutes, until he realized we had some distance to go. He threw it back at me.

"Hold your own jacket, man!" David had some dignity.

I charged down Main Street, pumping myself up. I could see a crowd of people two hundred yards away, and Justin was in the middle of them. This was it. No hesitation, no resistance. Just walk up and nail the cocksucker. Pound that fucker into the ground. Hit him first and keep hitting for as long as I can. That was my only chance. As I got closer, I dropped my jacket, my vision began to glaze over, to blur slightly, and I knew that I was going into fight mode. But within five feet of the asshole, I felt hands on my chest and shoulders.

People were saying, "Wait. Not here, man."

They pointed to an empty lot next to the hardware store, where the ground was barren and gravelly. There were a couple trucks parked there and the hardware store was open. They knew me. That's where I'd gotten my hunting license renewed every year, where Dad sent me for nails and other supplies for his projects.

Somebody's bound to call the cops, I thought. Justin had already started in that direction. His shirt was off. He was pale and skinny, as I said, like he was still suffering from the potato famine. But I knew what kind of ass-whupping power the bastard had. I had to hit first, or I'd never survive.

Justin rolled his head around and flexed his neck muscles. I charged, and before I could land a single punch—

He got me square in the face. I reeled. He flurried like his brother, but these were fast, measured, hard blows. There was nothing I could do. I had no opportunities. I lost my footing in the gravel and went down on one knee. My hands went out for support, and he landed one final shot, a closed-fist backhanded shot right in the center of my face. My nose popped, cartilage shattered, and blood gushed out. I didn't know I was capable of bleeding that much.

Justin still had ahold of my shirt and yelled, "Is that it?! Are you finished?"

I spat through a face full of blood. "Yeah, I'm finished."

He let me go. I steadied myself with one hand and clutched my nose with the other. The blood was soaking my chest and the ground.

His brother, Norton, appeared out of nowhere in a rage and towered over me. He was like a dog riled up by the sight of blood. He said, "You wanted to fight me. You wanna fight me now, motherfucker? Come on, is that what you want? Finish him off, Justin! Kick his fucking head in"—and he pulled his leg back as if he were about to do it himself. What a disgusting human being, I thought. I just hope he doesn't kick me. But Justin shoved his brother back and screamed at him to shut the fuck up. Then he stood before me and extended his hand. I took it, and he helped me to my feet.

"Everything's cool, then?" he said.

I nodded. Every time I breathed, I shot a spray of blood into the air in front of me. I speckled his face with blood, but he pretended not to notice.

[THIRTY-THREE]

Dicky was never getting out of jail. His bail was something like a million dollars and there was no way his mother could come up with collateral for that. He was stuck until he was sentenced, just like me. So I saw him every day, even though we weren't cellmates. We went to rec together.

The rec yard was a sixty-foot-long, thirty-foot-wide courtyard with a concrete floor and twenty-five-foot-high stone walls all the way around it. Stretched over the top of it was chain-link fencing, and around the tops of the walls was razor wire. There were two wrought-iron benches coated in rubber against a wall, and two basketball hoops, one at either end of the yard.

We seldom played real basketball games. That required too much effort. When you sit in a jail cell for twenty-three hours a day, you get fat and lazy. I had put on fifteen pounds, and when I sat down on the toilet my thighs touched each other for the first time in my life. We played HORSE. It required no gymnastics, and it held our attention.

"So, I'm reading about serial killers," I told Dicky. The guard sat inside the door to the rec yard, so he couldn't hear what we were talking about.

"Yeah?" he asked. "Which ones?" He stood facing me with both his wrists limp and his mouth agape with his tongue over his lower teeth. "You got an H *and* an O?" he asked.

"Yeah." I walked to where the ball was rolling slowly away from the wall, stooped down, and picked it up. "All of them," I said. "Bundy, Gacy, Dahmer. What do you think about all that?" I took aim at the basket, shot, and missed. "Serial killers and shit."

Dicky retrieved the ball, just as slowly as I did. "Well," he said, nodding his head, "I say, if it feels good, do it."

"Really?" I looked up at the sky through the fencing. It was the only time we ever got to see blue sky. "That's kind of fucked up, man."

He lifted the ball up and grinned. "*Everything's* fucked up." He shot. Missed. The ball bounced off the wall and rolled back to him. He picked it up and threw it to me.

I caught the ball. I looked at him. "You killed that old lady, didn't you?"

"I told you," he said. "My buddy did it."

I nodded, tried to do a hook shot. "That's so fucked up," I said.

"Yeah, so are you."

"Not that fucked up," I said.

He laughed. "Right." He followed the ball and stopped just over it, looked back at me, and said, "Give it time. You're halfway there."

He picked up the ball and took aim. I watched him.

"What the fuck are you talking about?" I said.

He looked at me, smiled. "Nothing at all, man."

[THIRTY-FOUR]

Sixteen was a significant year. All the really important things in my life, the explosions, the catastrophic events, all started unfolding—rehab, the fire in the school, the arrests, Joan, the robbery, the high-speed chase, jail. Like dominoes falling, like an algebra problem being worked out.

My mom and dad always went to bed around eleven, and when I felt it reasonably safe, I'd sneak out and walk up to the pizza shop. On this night it was particularly busy, and when I walked through the front door Mickey Bowen yelled something at me about how pissed off I was about to be.

Charlie Bender stopped me by the pinball machine and said, "That Mindy bitch is your girlfriend, Nate?"

I had met Mindy very recently through another girl who'd said Mindy would put out. Mindy was kind of ugly, and she was stupid, but I didn't have any other options. So I talked to her a few times, and we even kissed once, kind of—a half-assed kiss—so yeah, I thought I had enough reason to consider her my girlfriend.

I nodded. "Why?"

"Dude, we saw her down at the ballpark fucking around with a bunch of guys. Word is she sucked off about six dudes."

"What the fuck are you talking about?" I was confused. It was too much to wrap my head around.

"Yeah," Charlie said. "It's true, man. I'm sorry." I nodded and lit a smoke and went into the back room, leaned against a wall, and pretended to watch a couple of guys shoot a game of pool. Could this be true? It could be.

Just then Charlie yelled, "Nate, you sneak out again?"

I yelled, "Yeah, why?"

"Your dad's here."

I went out front, and sure enough Dad was coming by the front windows. He opened the front door, spotted me, and snarled, "Come on!"

I walked down the sidewalk in front of him as he was saying, "Can't fuckin' trust you, can I? Can't fuckin' trust you at all."

I wanted to turn around and bash his head in. When we got in the front door of our house, he shoved me. I stayed as firm as I could and turned around.

He said, "Oh, you want to fight? You think you can whip me? Anytime you fucking want, boy!"

I didn't. I knew he could still knock the shit out of me.

— — —

Flipping off the world became a drug for me. I realized that authority was an illusion that required participation from both parties. If one party (the controlled) refused to play along, the other party (the controller) would lose their balance, drop the ball, get confused. In that window before they figured out how to regain their power, you were absolutely free. During class, while the teacher lectured, I'd get up and go over to the window, look outside, daydream, because I could. When the teacher told me to return to my seat, I'd refuse, because I could. When they told me to go to the office, I'd go outside, go into the woods, smoke a cigarette. Then I'd go to my next class. The principal would call me over the PA, and I'd go pay him a visit. He'd suspend me, call my parents, send me home.

If Mom and Dad grounded me for two weeks because of my suspension, I'd go upstairs, cut through the storage room, climb out the window, slide down the side of the house, and walk uptown. I would say to myself, "I can do *anything* I want." I had no limits. If I observed limits, it was because I consented to those limits, only because defying them wasn't worth the hassle. I always knew what the consequences would be. I knew the disciplinary schedule at school. Ten detentions before you got a Saturday school, five Saturday schools before you got a three-day in-school suspension. Two three-days before you got a ten-day. Then it's out-of-school suspension. Two three-days, then a ten-day. Two ten-days, then expulsion. I was proud that up until this point I had been given everything except expulsion, and expulsion would come. I was exhausting the disciplinary schedule.

In school, I always knew what to expect. It was the legal system I wasn't prepared for. When I set the fire in school and was sent to the juvie jail, I was surprised. It was a miserable, nightmare place, and it was clear that now I had moved beyond an environment where authority perhaps hoped for a better solution. I had moved into an environment where authority punished with a crushing indifference. When I went to real jail, when I was facing prison, this was even more obvious. The legal system doesn't wear kid gloves. The legal system doesn't care. The legal system was an authority that wasn't going to get confused when I refused to play along. The legal system never gets confused. So juvie surprised me, and jail shocked me.

— — —

Before jail, before the fire, my mom took me to see a counselor in Beckettstown. He was a Jewish guy named Herman with long, high frizzy hair and big, bushy sideburns. He thought if he acted and dressed hip, he'd have a better chance of connecting with the juvenile delinquents who came to see him, so he wore a biker wallet with a chain like mine, which contrasted nicely with his white shirt and necktie. He brought in a switchblade one day to show me. So I pulled mine out and we compared knives. He was really a decent guy, highly complimentary. He said he was impressed with my use of language. He said I was wonderfully noncommittal.

I explained to him my philosophy of Satanism, which was really a very simple inversion of Christian ideology: "If you're a God-fearing asshole and you do everything you can to please your little god, but you fuck up and piss him off, you'll go to hell and it'll suck. If you're a Satanist and you've allied yourself with Satan, well, of course you'll go to hell, but you will have earned Satan's respect and then hell won't be such a bad place at all—in fact it'll probably be more like a paradise."

Herman tried very hard to get me to see where my self-destructive path would probably lead me, but it didn't do much good. Eventually he referred me to a colleague, a middle-aged female counselor who let me smoke in her office. As you can imagine, I thought she was a real pal. I told her about the fights I'd had at school. Philip and I had recently figured out how to huff gas—how to inhale the fumes from a small container of gasoline to get high—and we'd started to do that a lot, so I told her about that. I told her I'd tried some diet pills I got from a kid at school, but all they did was make me irritable. She suggested to my parents that rehabilitation was what I needed.

When my parents talked to me about it, I was all for it. Goddamn, a vacation from my fucking parents was indeed exactly what I needed.

"How soon can I go?" I asked.

"Two weeks," Mom said. She looked like she was about to cry.

— — —

A couple of days later I was sitting in school and thinking, "Jesus, I don't know if I can take this for two more weeks," when a brilliant idea occurred to me. Beat somebody's ass and get a ten-day suspension. That should take me right up to when I'm supposed to go. I was sitting up on the bleachers in the gym with a group of hoods: Charlie Bender, Jared Hopkins, Mickey Bowen, Rich Bass, and Tommy James. But who am I going to beat up? Who deserves it most?

Well, there was always Roger.

Roger came to the doorway of the gym and leaned against the jamb, hands in his pockets, all nonchalant, all badass like he ran the fucking place—blue sweater, white turtleneck underneath, his hair finely sculpted into what looked like a diving board protruding from his forehead. Every time I saw the kid he lifted his hands and did a backward nod with his head, a nonverbal challenge—asking me if I want a piece. About half an hour before this in the cafeteria he gave me this little ritualized *fuck you* again. This was of course why he came to mind.

I said to Tommy, "I'm about to kick Roger's ass."

"Really? You are?" Tommy was not really a badass himself, but he hung out with the badasses, so the reputation sort of rubbed off on him.

I told him to hold my jacket, I took off some bracelets, and when I saw the prick at the doorway, I started down the bleachers. I walked straight toward him, and as he got closer and closer, things began to get blurry—I disengaged from reality. I said nothing to him. I didn't pause for a second. As soon as he was within reach, I let him have it as hard as I could on his left cheek. He clutched his face and doubled over to his right; I kicked him in the stomach, threw him around the hallway from wall to wall, landing punches every time I brought him to a stop, until Mr. Denoon grabbed me with both hands and threw me with shocking force away from Roger. I regained my balance and started back toward Roger, who was bleeding a little from his nose and whose face was puffing up. I yelled, "You got a fuckin' problem, bitch?"

Denoon dragged me down to the principal's office. Ten-day vacation, and next time, Mr. Henry, we're calling the police to charge you with assault.

Thank you very much, Mr. Callander. That is perfectly acceptable.

[THIRTY-FIVE]

P-21. Every day those crazies from the mental health block filed past my door on their way down to rec, and every day that guy Earl, the craziest of them, paused in front of my door and looked in at me. He leered, with this I-want-to-fuck-your-corpse grin on his face. After the second time he did this, I went up and stood right in front of the door and stared back. The fact that I was four inches from his face didn't affect his expression.

The next time he did it, I said, "Earl, what's your fucking problem?"

"I got no problem, inmate."

"How about I cut your fucking head off, Earl?"

He smirked. "You think you can do that?"

"Positive, cocksucker."

He smirked again and walked away. God, I wanted to beat his ass.

I had to go inside the cell block for hot water. Once

inside, nothing would separate me from Earl. He'd have no protection. Sure, he was bigger than me, but he was old and slow. I couldn't be sure how slow. He probably wasn't slow enough. As far as I knew, Earl could have been a true psychopath. He could very well truly be exactly what I was afraid I was becoming. Then I was terrified. What if he was planning on attacking me? And what if he had a real shank? Some little piece of hand-made cutlery he'd been grinding away at for as long as he'd been here? Fuck. But I had to go in there. I needed hot water.

I dropped a bar of soap down a sock and swung it against my bunk. There was a heavy thud. I'd rather have a piece of steel, but this might do. Well, if Earl was a threat, and he sure as shit looked like he was, then I'd have to take him out, and fast. If I could make it to the hot water spigot and fill my cup, I could scald his face first, then pound him with the soap sock.

Next time he came by, I didn't say anything to him. I just looked into his eyes when he came to my window and imagined smashing his face in. When they were all locked up in their cell block, I took my soap sock, hid it in my waistband, and called a guard. My heart was pounding. I was getting short of breath. I could feel my adrenaline amping up. I couldn't tell if this felt good or not. It was familiar, though.

Josh came to my door. "Hot water?" he asked.

"Yeah." And I showed him my cup.

He opened my door and I went out. He opened the door to the cell block and I went in. He didn't even follow me. He stayed in the doorway and talked to another inmate. Why would he watch me? I'd never given any of the guards any reason to worry. I scanned the dayroom. Earl was nowhere to be seen. I went to the hot water spigot and filled my cup. I looked around again. No Earl. Where the fuck was he?

"Come on, Nate." It was Josh. I turned to him. "I got rounds to do, man."

I left the cell block and went into my own cell. Then the insanity of it all nearly split me in half. I had less than three months to go, and I'd be out for good. Less than three months, and I'd already been inside for over nine months, and I was going to throw it all away, get my ass charged with assault with a deadly weapon, get my probation revoked, and get shipped straight to prison for six fucking years. *What the fuck was wrong with me?*

"Josh," I said, before he slammed my door.

"What?"

"I gotta get out of this cell. There's no window to the outside. I never know what time it is. I'm going fucking crazy, man."

"I'll see what I can do." He shut my door.

"I'm serious, Josh. I'm losing it."

He nodded and walked away.

From then on, whenever the guys in the cell block were taken to rec, I just placed a sheet of paper over the window to my cell door and waited for them to pass.

[THIRTY-SIX]

The rehab place was called the Charinton Institute for Behavioral Health. It was in a town called Charinton, fifty miles west of Brickville. The counselors were all right, but they immediately drugged me. I was on three different kinds of medication from the moment I walked in the door. I couldn't think. I knew where I was only after a bit of concentration. Usually I didn't care where I was. I hated that fucking place, and I was afraid they were trying to kill me. I called Mom and told her I didn't want to be there, but she said I had to stay. And I could smoke only six cigarettes a day. It was the worst place on earth.

That was the first time I'd ever experienced real institutional control. Really the first time I faced the absolute indifference of people who could tell me what to do and punish me if I didn't listen—who might have even been excited about the possibility of punishing me, without giving any damn about how I felt.

At first I was resistant. "I don't want to take the fucking meds. I want a cigarette."

The cold, cruel, unmovable response from the nurse was, "You *will* take this medication, one way or another."

I knew she was right. So almost immediately I accepted what I was up against—I was up against a machine that didn't care how much I struggled; if I wanted to struggle, it would still have its way. This is the same thing I recognized and accepted when I went to jail. There is nothing to be gained by fighting something you can't possibly beat.

I got a cold as soon as I got there. I was congested. I couldn't breathe. On top of that, the meds destroyed my ability to think. A few days later I was feeling slightly better, and by the end of the week I could function. I still felt removed from reality. I was slow to respond.

There was a kid in the room next door to me who snuck cigarettes in. He asked me if I wanted to smoke one with him in the bathroom. If we got caught, we'd probably lose all our smoking privileges. I said, "Man, I just want to do my time and get the fuck outta here." So that was what I did. I did my time.

That same kid found out that if you tried to run, the counselors would chase you down and shoot you up with something that fucked you up for days. He wanted to find out if the stuff was any good, so one day when we were walking from one building to another in single file, he broke and ran like hell. Two big counselors tackled him before he got fifty feet away, and they dragged him inside. A couple of days later, I asked him what the shot was like.

"It fucking sucked," he said, looking like he wanted to puke.

There was an insane girl in there, Cody, who had a nice body; in fact, she was damn near perfect. She got into the habit of rubbing my dick through my pants under the table we all sat around in group therapy. She wanted me to sneak down to her room after lights out and fuck her, but I didn't have the energy for it. Besides, the meds I was on rendered my dick completely useless. She said I looked just like her boyfriend. She said she wanted to jam a pencil into the therapist's neck and burn the whole place down.

On the night Cody disappeared, I woke up in my bed and couldn't move. I was paralyzed. It seemed like I lay there forever, terrified, thinking maybe this happened every night, maybe they put us into this state and did strange experiments on us. While I lay there, panicking, I thought I could hear Cody in the next room, throwing chairs against the walls, fighting off half a dozen orderlies. This was the most crazed, cornered-animal moment of Cody's life; there were walls of fire all around the room one moment, and scorching fires inside her head the next. I felt that I was personally responsible for what was happening to her, that another innocent's life was coming to an ugly end because of something I did or didn't do. I eventually fell back asleep, but the next morning Cody didn't show up in the smoking room, and she wasn't in group. When I asked about her, they said she'd been discharged. I asked, "Was there some kind of fight last night?" I never got a straight answer out of them.

There was another girl who wanted me to sneak into her room at night and fuck her. Her name was Lynelle. She had short dyed-red hair and blue eyes. They took us all in a bus to a skating rink, and she and I sat together in a booth the whole time, touching each other under the table. She was much saner than Cody, but not as good-looking. Cody was beautiful with a dangerous, wild-animal beauty while Lynelle was just pretty. She was smarter; she talked about how the therapists were trying to reprogram us, trying to rewire us into cooperative slaves. She said her plan was to agree with everything they said, to convince them that she was benefiting from their work, and then, when they let her go, she was going to shoot herself in the head with her father's shotgun as soon as she got home. This was so sexy to me and I can't tell you why.

There was a dayroom with a television and a few sofas, where we could be entertained if we'd gotten enough work done, if we'd really shown a desire to get better. Our reward for the desire for self-betterment was two hours of trash talk shows and mindless comedy. Lynelle and I were in the dayroom alone—first time we'd been completely alone. We kissed. An orderly ran in and pulled her off me, literally lifted her into the air and threw her across the room, bruising her arm. It was unbelievable really, as if he were saving my life, as if a little kiss were the absolute worst thing that could happen to someone. So we were no longer allowed to be within fifteen feet of each other, Lynelle and I. They were saving us from each other.

[THIRTY-SEVEN]

I sat out in the hallway with Kline one night while he did his paperwork. It wasn't all that uncommon for the guards to allow this—not with me anyway. I appreciated the time out of my cell, and they didn't seem to mind the company.

On every floor in the main hallway there was a giant steel office desk and two wheeled chairs, one in front of the desk and one beside it, its back facing the wall. I sat in the one with the back to the wall.

"Kline, how many homicidal maniacs have you had in here?"

Kline leaned back in his chair, put his hands behind his head, and gazed up at the wall. "Let's see." He squinted. Finally, he just said, "A few. Why?"

"Were they all obviously insane? I mean, could you have a conversation with them?"

"By 'homicidal maniac,' what exactly do you mean?"

"I mean torture killers. Not these fucks that rob people and blow their brains out. I mean sadistic motherfuckers, like serial killers. The sons of bitches that like it."

"We haven't had many of those. There was one guy who killed some kids. He was an all right guy. Never had any trouble out of him."

"Was he bright?"

"Sure, bright enough."

"Was he interesting?"

Kline looked at me, turned skeptical. "Why are you asking these things?"

I threw up a hand and let it fall in my lap. "Just curious. Been reading about serial killers."

After that conversation with Dicky, I couldn't stop thinking about it. He'd gotten to me. Halfway there? I'm practically a killer? That's what he was saying. Was he right? Was I more fucked up than I thought? Was it inevitable that I would someday snap, go completely nuts, slaughter people? This terrified me. I mean, maybe after everything, after all this, coupled with whatever the hell was already in me . . .

Billy the Kid is one thing; Jeffrey Dahmer is another.

"Well, look, Nate. From what I've seen, there's no way to tell. You can't call a man as a baby killer from ten feet away any quicker than you can call a man as a garbage collector. It's just not that simple. Not even after talking to them for a while. Maybe if you were a trained psychologist or something, and even then I don't think it's possible."

So there was no way to know. I could be a psychotic bastard, the kind of psychotic bastard who'd cut open his own mother and sniff her intestines—and I wouldn't even know. It could just come out of me one day, a brand-new personality trait, intact and ready for action, before there was anything I could do about it. Maybe that's what was happening. Maybe it was coming out now.

I sat in my cell with thoughts of murder creeping into me every ten minutes. I'd try to read, and suddenly in the middle of an engaging paragraph I'd have this vision of myself driving a knife into somebody's forehead, scraping it around and scrambling brains. I'd start to sweat. Fuck, I really didn't want to be one of those sick bastards. Rampage killers, assassins, gangsters—those are all right. A total degenerate who can't help himself is another thing entirely. I had to get ahold of myself.

[THIRTY-EIGHT]

On Christmas Day in the early morning Dad picked me up at rehab, Charinton, the nuthouse. I wasn't being released for good, but I was allowed to leave for the day. Dad was happy to see me. He brought me a bottle of apple juice, had it in the cooler full of pop he always carried with him. The apple juice made me sick. It looked like urine. I couldn't stop thinking of drinking urine. I was still feeling dopey. I was still slow, but Dad talked a lot and I didn't mind listening.

"I've been working on the lawn mower," he said. "Got it running. It was a bad carburetor."

"Hmm."

"You remember that trash can I made last year? The wooden one with the lid on hinges? I think I'm gonna make some more and try to sell them. Maybe twenty-five, thirty bucks each."

"Hmm."

"You remember Jake? Owns that gas station out by Shoshone? He'll let me sell them there."

"Hmm. Yeah. Sounds good."

When we got home Dad set up the video camera and made us get down in front of the tree on our knees. He handed us presents and directed us on how we should open them in a cinematically pleasing way. It was annoying because Dad wasn't sure how he wanted it to look. He kept moving the tree, made Mom hold up a white sheet behind us blocking out the tree, even made us rewrap some of the presents to do them over again because we'd fucked it up the first time. Due to my drugged state, I was pretty docile, but my brother was infuriated. Finally he blew up.

"Jesus Christ, Dad, just unplug the damn camera and let us open our fucking gifts!"

This was the end of it. Dad flew into a rage. They screamed at each other, and Mom tried to intervene. Christmas was in shambles. It was chaos. I pulled my jacket on and walked out the door, saying, "Call me when you want to have Christmas. I'm going to Philip's." They didn't even notice.

It was eight o'clock in the morning and the streets were deserted. There wasn't anyone in sight. There was a bit of snow on the ground, but not much, just enough to crunch under my feet. I walked slowly because my boots were slick. My spurs clanked in the quiet. I made my way down the street, smoking, unable to think much of anything.

Charlie Bender's older brother—I can't remember his name—drove by and stopped his car. He backed up and rolled his window down. "Nate, what's up?" he said.

"Just walking, man."

"I heard you were locked up in some mental hospital." He scratched his goatee and tipped his baseball hat back a bit.

"I am." I lit a cigarette and leaned against the car. "I'm out for today. Christmas."

He nodded. "You need a ride?"

"Sure."

"Get in." And he gave me a ride out to Philip's house.

I knocked on Philip's door and he opened it. "Nate!" He was genuinely happy to see me. He hugged me. I wasn't exactly happy to see him. I wasn't unhappy about it. I just didn't feel anything. The house was strangely empty.

"Where is everybody?" I asked.

"Mom made everybody go to church."

"How'd you get out of it?"

He shrugged and gave a mischievous grin. Philip and I sat on the front porch and talked. I told him about Cody and Lynelle.

"But," I said, "dude, for some reason I can't even get hard most of the time. And, listen, when I did get hard the other day, I jerked off, but when I came, nothing came out."

"What the fuck?" He was horrified.

"I know."

About a half an hour later my dad pulled into the driveway and came to the porch. He said merry Christmas to Philip, and we left.

"I'm sorry," he said as we drove.

"It's okay."

"I'm really glad you're here," he said. "I just thought it'd be nice to get it on video. I didn't mean for it to turn out this way."

"It's fine." And I meant it. I wasn't really upset about any of it. I hadn't even been all that upset when I left. I just didn't feel like being around for a fight.

Christmas was all right after that. I got home and Jim apologized, and Mom said she loved me and everything was fine. We had a great time. Dad put the camera away. We laughed about the whole gift-opening fiasco, we joked about how I was now classifiable as a mental defective, and finally we ate canned ham and mashed potatoes. Then I went back to the lunatic asylum, was strip-searched, and put to bed.

[THIRTY-NINE]

I was left in P-21 for a month. Like I said, there was no window. It was cold. I never knew whether it was day or night.

I read.

It came to me that I wanted to be a holy man of some kind. I wanted to be a monk. I wanted to pursue the truth, some kind of truth, at all costs. I didn't know how this might be done. There was the witchcraft of course, but I'd gotten a lot of witchcraft books from the library cart and it had all begun to look very childish. It became pretty clear to me there was nothing scientific about it, that there was no good reason to believe that it worked. I thought about studying my Bible—and I tried. I started to think about getting out and being a holy man in the world, and what that might be like. Travel from one Christian revival to another, spreading the Word. Be like those oily preachers or, at best, like some slick phony in a

Lincoln laying down a routine for country rubes. What a nightmare. I thought about going up into the mountains and meditating, about becoming a Zen master.

I didn't know what I wanted to do, or what I wanted to be. I wondered how one ever knows what one wants, or what one *should* be. I wondered if there was a difference between naturally becoming something and *wanting* to become something. I had wanted to be a criminal, and I became one. I had wanted to be a hoodlum—I'd worked hard at that—and I succeeded. Now I wanted to be an artist, or a holy man, a holy artist maybe. Again, is there a difference between wanting and being?

Is it worth being if I have to *want* to be it? I asked myself. What is the difference between natural and artificial when it comes to motivation and interest, desire? This question began to obsess me. What's phony and what's not? What is an identity? What's beneath it all?

I couldn't say. But I needed to know.

I couldn't let go of it. The question wrapped itself around my brain and constricted. I locked up. I couldn't think about anything else. This went on for days and days. I woke up to the question, and I wrestled sleep from the question. It was the strangest obsession that I had ever experienced.

I had been reading *Tristessa*, by Jack Kerouac, and *Interview with the Vampire*, by Anne Rice. Heroin addiction in Mexico City and immortal vampires roaming the earth for centuries without a trace of the divine. *There is no God.* This is what these books said to me. *There is no devil, no demons or omens. You might be wrong about everything.*

I was working my way into the first real depression of my fully conscious adult life. This was a crisis, and I could find no solution. The question eventually broadened to include all questions, and no questions. It became this general sense of being bound up by uncertainty, and beneath the uncertainty, terror—a feeling that I absolutely had to come to some kind of conclusion about everything, I had to set everything right and know something about myself in the world for certain, or it would all fall out from underneath me, and I didn't know how I could live after that.

The agony of having a mind in a rock-solid knot reached an intolerable point—I don't remember the date, or what time it was, or what was going on aside from those books I was reading—but at a certain point, when I thought I couldn't take it any longer, when I paced my cell feverishly and would have looked to any observer like a total madman, I somehow stopped, and the knot broke, it thawed, and I just gave up. I let go. I couldn't go on. I couldn't sustain the tension.

I stopped thinking and I fell asleep, and when I woke up, something truly amazing had happened. I looked at the world as if I were seeing it for the first time. I had new eyes. Not just that. The *world* was new. It was a solid place, vivid, more real than it had ever seemed. And it all made perfect sense. It was . . . just what it was, without explanation, without theory. It needed nothing. It was perfect.

There were no ghosts in this world. There was no magic. There was life, and the Earth, and the Universe.

Electrons, protons, and dark matter. There were human beings, and their experiences, and their inventions. There were thoughts, and things. And it was all Reality, a solid thing, an obvious thing, more obvious than I could ever have imagined, trapped as I'd been playing childish games. In Reality, thought was thought, movement was movement, and matter was matter. In Reality, there was no need for questions of identity. I was what I was, always.

After this I began to call civilization—everything about it, all its ideas, all its constructions, clothes, houses, morals, bibles, literature, poetry, jails—the Grand Human Invention. I imagined it springing naturally from the Earth, as natural as trees, or groundhogs, or the planet itself. I imagined myself springing naturally from the Earth, and imagined all my imaginations springing naturally from me.

The difference between natural and artificial? Phony and genuine? Real and unreal? What was beneath identity? It was all natural, all necessary, all the same thing. And it was all perfect.

[FORTY]

When I got out of rehab at the Charinton Institute for Behavioral Health, I was committed to a better life. I really was. It wasn't that they had reprogrammed me. It was that the counselors had mediated a truce between my parents and me.

Several weeks before the issue of the hospital ever came up, I had approached my parents with a list of liberties that I thought it appropriate that I enjoy. They included the liberty to visit the pizza shop or to visit friends, provided I do some chores around the house. This was a huge issue of contention. When I first got to Charinton and one of the counselors asked my mom what kind of kids I ran with, she responded smugly, "We don't allow him to *run*."

The counselor said, "You do realize it's good for kids to be around people their own age, right?"

By the time I left Charinton, I had everything on

that list, provided I got good grades and did some chores. I was fine with this. I was intent on a new lifestyle. Give and take. Compromise. It's the only way things get done.

Life had potential, it had meaning, there was a logic to it, and I had my part—and I felt great about this—but within two months I'd be losing my mind and setting the principal's office on fire, then lying on a concrete bunk in juvie wondering what the fuck had gone wrong.

I left the hospital on New Year's Day with a two-month supply of bupropion and Mellaril. Mellaril is a powerful sedative like thorazine, and bupropion is a heavy-duty antidepressant. They didn't tell my parents or me what these drugs were and they didn't tell us that I shouldn't stop taking them abruptly. They didn't tell us to continue with the prescriptions. They just gave us the pills and sent me on my way. As far as we knew, they could have been antibiotics. They may have told us to follow up with our family doctor, but it doesn't seem like they did—either way, our confusion about the meds was a disaster waiting to happen.

There is a whole series of interesting events that I have always thought were disconnected. Only years later would it become clear to me that all of them were directly related to the drugs. I've tried bupropion since and had a horrible experience. Granted, I've done a lot of other drugs that have primed me for psychosis, namely meth-amphetamine, the most evil shit on earth, but the bupropion brought on a full-blown break with reality. I took it for a week and had to stop, or I would've lost my mind.

They did not tell us at the hospital that I couldn't stop cold turkey. It'll bring on psychosis.

So I took that month's worth of pills and that was it. By the end of February, I had set a fire in my school, gone to jail, and been placed under house arrest.

For that first medicated month, things went well. I did my homework, got As and Bs, hung out at the pizza shop, and generally enjoyed life. I drank some beers with Philip one night and got considerably drunk on just two beers. Of course it was the pills. Even Philip said at the time, "Man, you shouldn't be this drunk on two beers."

Then Philip and I are out in the driveway. I'm leaning against the station wagon. Philip hands me the gas can and I inhale quickly a dozen times, hold my breath, and pass the can to Philip. I'm enveloped in a warm, disorienting narcotic swoon, and there's an intense rhythmic chiming inside my head. I lose all feeling in my body, slide down the fender of the car, and hit the gravel. Everything happens three times. I slide away from the car three times, hit the ground three times, and Philip asks if I'm all right three times. Strangest experience of my life—it's never happened again on any other drug. This, too, was probably because of the pills. Gas never did anything like this to me before. Nothing has.

Around then was the first time I got laid. This was sometime in early February. I always thought the more embarrassing aspects of the experience were a matter of inadequacy, but they weren't. It was probably the pills too.

One Saturday afternoon Philip and I were walking around and saw Heidi, a girl I knew from school, and two girls we didn't recognize sitting out in front of Heidi's house on lawn chairs. We stopped and sat down. Heidi introduced the girls and said they were from Beckettstown, another town about a half an hour away, much larger, practically a city. One girl was called Patty. She said she was a madam and the other girl was one of her whores. The other girl didn't seem to mind. It might have been true. Patty talked about making good money giving blowjobs at the bars in Beckettstown—she said she knew exactly how to get a guy off quick. "You suck like hell and jack the balls while you're doing it," she said. "Makes them come in two minutes."

I said, "I've never had a blowjob." I don't know why I said this. It's an incredibly uncool thing to say.

"You want one?" she asked. "I'll take you around to the back porch and suck you off right now."

I think my heart stopped. I blushed. I said, "Maybe later."

Philip and I left soon after.

Philip said, "What the hell's wrong with you, man?"

I played it off like I thought she was ugly, but honestly I couldn't answer his question. Next day at school, I asked Heidi for Patty's number. I had pumped myself up, argued with myself, reasoned it through, and knew that I couldn't miss this opportunity. That night I called her, and she invited me to her house that weekend.

Patty lived with her great-aunt in a dumpy little trailer in a trailer park crammed with dumpy little trailers that stank like cat piss and was full of squawking caged birds. My mom and dad dropped me off and went back into town to do some shopping. They thought I was taking Patty to a movie. I hoped we would stay home instead. I went inside and Patty introduced me to her great-aunt, who was an invalid—terribly skinny, practically skeletal, so fragile she couldn't get out of the chair and, judging by the debris around the chair and the close proximity of the TV (within arms' reach), looked like she hadn't gotten out of the chair in ten years. There was probably a bedpan nearby.

Patty took me to her room and handed me something.

"My aunt wants you to have this," she said.

I looked at it. It was a walnut that had been partially cracked open and stuffed with a condom. It was the most absurd thing I'd ever seen. I shoved it in my pocket and took my jacket off, sat down beside Patty on the bed. She put on some music. The other girl from Heidi's house was there; she was apparently her sister, and they shared the same room. Her sister lay on her bed reading a magazine, listening to music through headphones.

I didn't know what the hell to do. We sat and smoked for a long time. When she realized that I wasn't about to make a move, she kissed me. This was my second kiss. My first kiss, with Amy, the crazy girl, blew my brains out. This one was disappointing, to say the least. She did strange things with her teeth. She took her T-shirt off and lay back, unfastening her bra. She had giant tits with red marks on them from the bra and big brown nipples. I moved on top of her, and started licking and sucking. I did this for forever, half an hour, an hour. I would have gone on sucking her tits for the rest of my life. Not because I enjoyed it so much but because I didn't know what else to do. She finally said something and I looked up.

"I'm going to take my pants off," she said. I stood up. "Turn around and look the other way," she said. "I'm self-conscious about my body."

I did as I was told.

I stood there staring in the opposite direction, my heart pounding and my hands shaking. Sex, at this moment, was the absolute last thing on my mind. I was terrified. She said okay, and when I turned around, she was under the blanket.

She said, "Take your pants off and climb under here with me." I did it, trembling. Sliding under the blanket and lying on top of her, I wondered if everyone was this terrified the first time. They didn't seem to be in the movies. I went back to licking her tits and she played with me. But nothing happened. She continued to play with me, to rub me around on her pussy, but still nothing happened. She said, "It's okay, this is normal." We went on like this for another half hour.

"Is this still normal?" I asked.

"No," she said.

Finally she got me hard enough to enter, and I did. I didn't feel anything. I started moving my hips rhythmically, but still didn't feel anything. She moved around, she moaned, I moved, and finally I stopped.

She said, "Did you come?"

"I think so." To be honest, I didn't. I didn't feel

anything except her pubic hair prickling my balls. This I do remember feeling, but nothing else.

So that was my first experience with sex. Regardless of how disastrous or disappointing it was, I strutted around the next day like a stud with genuine pussy juice on my dick, and I didn't wash all day. I told Philip that it had been amazing and that I was now addicted to pussy. I'd occasionally go into the bathroom just to feel myself, to make sure it had really happened.

[FORTY-ONE]

I talked to Philip a few times on the phone while I was in jail. It always felt strange. I normally felt that the outside world was somehow put on hold, that everything had somehow frozen and would be waiting for me just the way it had been when I went into jail. Hearing his voice sucked me back out into reality.

Philip said, "Joan's been back around here."

Shit, Joan. I could suddenly see her face very clearly. She had a small birthmark on her neck. I had forgotten about the birthmark.

"I don't give a shit," I said.

"Oh, you're going to."

"Why?"

"I heard she's got a kid," he said quickly. He waited for me to reply.

I didn't. I just sat on my bunk and stared at the floor, trying to imagine what it could mean.

Philip continued, "I keep hearing it's yours."

I still didn't say anything. A couple of months before Joan had left me, we thought she might have been pregnant. She got a test and she said it was negative. Nobody ever saw the test but her. She could have been pregnant, she could have been lying, she could've gotten pregnant right after she left. How could I know?

"You there?" he asked, after a few seconds of silence.

"Yeah," I said. "I'm here." Everybody had known about it. Mom and Dad knew she might be pregnant. I had wanted her to be pregnant. I was excited. I told my brother that it felt like—get this—Christmas. Now, in my cell, I felt like such an idiot. A baby would have been the absolute last thing I needed.

"We should've fucking killed her," Philip said. He was just going along with what he thought I might have been thinking. He did this a lot.

"Don't say that," I said. I remembered making love to her. I remembered her brown eyes. I remembered how I felt I couldn't live without her. I was *desperate* with her.

"I heard her brother's out to get you when you get out of there."

I didn't want to talk anymore. I didn't want to hear about any idiotic drama. "Her brother's a pussy," I said dismissively.

"I know, but he's talking shit all over the place."

"I don't care!" I was getting frustrated. "You think it *is* my kid?"

"I don't know."

"It could be anybody's." I meant it. It really could be anybody's. But it could be mine too.

"It's not mine," he said. "I never fucked her."

"I know, man."

We hung up after a couple more awkward moments, and I went on thinking about Joan.

She was my first love affair. I was, in every sense of the word, *entangled* with her—it was really as if she were a part of me, and all that emotion, all that commitment was reciprocated—at least I believed it was. I didn't stop believing it even after she drove away—I had my fears and my suspicions, but those are easy to brush aside. It all became unbearably obvious soon enough: I decided to travel halfway across the country to shoot her in the head.

[FORTY-TWO]

I was sixteen and fresh out of the nuthouse (Charinton) when I saw Joan for the first time—she wore combat boots and a black leather trench coat. She carried a copy of Freud's *Totem and Taboo* as she walked into my fifth-period study hall. Her hair was a kind of neon blue with streaks of red in it. She sat in front of me.

"*Psst*. What are you reading?" I asked.

She held it up.

I showed her my *Say You Love Satan*.

She nodded approvingly.

I asked, "Are you into this?"

She said, "What, Satanism? Sure."

I said, "Let's get a smoke after study hall. I know where to go."

So after study hall I took her to the spot around the east wall of the building where we couldn't be seen. David was there, bitching about something or other, probably fretting over an imminent ass-whipping by some jock. Joan and I talked about Satanism, heavy metal music, and sex. I thought I had met my soul mate.

After school that night I saw Joan sitting down on one of the guardrails leading up to the bridge down the street from my house. She had her guitar with her, a little blue electric, and we jammed. I showed her some Metallica licks and she showed me some Guns N' Roses licks. I was smitten.

Hanging out around the stoop under the Roll of Honor mural one night with a group of the hoods, I heard somebody asked Charlie Bender if he'd fuck Joan. He said, "Hell, no! She's ugly as a fucking dog, man!"

"I know, man." Rich Bass made a puking sound. "Nasty."

I didn't agree, but I thought it wise to keep my mouth shut. I was fairly ambivalent about what they were saying. On the one hand, no one wants a girlfriend everybody thinks is ugly, but on the other hand, it didn't look like I had any competition, which was good. And after I did start dating her, nobody ever said another word about it.

Patty was calling me in the evenings, but I was losing interest. She revealed that she sang country music at honky-tonks on the weekends. This disgusted me. If she sang death metal, that would be one thing, but *country*? It was on Valentine's Day that Joan came to my house for the first time. I hadn't invited her. She just knocked on the door and we stood around on the sidewalk smoking and talking for a couple of hours.

A lot of time was spent on my stoop in those days.

Mickey Bowen used to come by and jam with me. Eventually a crowd would gather. My dad distrusted the kids I hung out with and wouldn't let them in the house, and rightfully so.

When Joan left that night and I went back inside, my mom said, "So who was the girl with the disturbing hair?"

"A friend," I replied.

That night I broke up with Patty and asked Joan to be my woman.

[FORTY-THREE]

GED classes were available for the inmates at the jail. They took place once a week in the law library. Though I already had my GED, I took the classes just to get out of my cell for a little while. This was the only time I interacted face-to-face with the adult inmates—that is, without a door or window separating us.

Ed had a shaved head and tattoos, and he was pretty. I think he was a biker. He asked me one day, "You still in a cell with that old-lady killer?"

"No," I said. "Haven't been in a long time."

"That little fucker do it?"

"I don't know. He says he didn't."

"What's your feeling?"

"I think maybe he did. I don't know."

He shook his head. "Fucking stupid."

A black guy sat next to him; I think his name was Kimball. Now, he was hard. Kimball gave you the sense he'd been there and back, and dropped a few bodies on the way. He was bald too. He said, "You ain't gotta kill no old lady like that. You just ain't got to do it."

Ed nodded and looked down at the table. "What I'm saying. Ain't necessary at all."

Kimball went on. "Little fucking psycho," he said with real disgust. "You kill a gangster, no problem. You kill a motherfucker you got a beef with on the street, no motherfucking problem. Little old lady ain't done nothing to you? Shit, man. I don't know how you bunked with that little bitch."

"I can't stand him," I said. "We only bunked for a little while; then I asked to have my own cell back."

"I broke into plenty houses," Ed said. "The people come home, all you gotta do is tie 'em up in the basement, take the shit, and leave. Nobody gotta get hurt."

"I heard that." Kimball crossed his arms and said, "Little punk better hope I don't see his ass out west."

"West" meant prison, the penitentiary. Paradise County Jail was in Thompsonville, Illinois, and Thompsonville was on the eastern edge of the state, so no matter where you went after you were sentenced, you were going west.

I thought about guys like Ed and Kimball breaking into people's houses. I imagined them breaking into Mom and Dad's house. I imagined them tying Mom up. The thought pissed me off. A lot of the guys in jail seemed to live that way. Armed robbers, home invaders. Seemed like they'd all done it dozens of times. And who knew what else they'd done? They'd probably been doing this shit their whole lives. That's all they knew. Rob a house, go to jail, go west, get out, rob another house, go to jail . . . Jesus, I thought. All those people, all those victims . . . A normal person might never be the same after an experience like that, but to them, it was just all part of a day's work. They didn't feel anything for their victims. They didn't particularly dislike them or want to hurt them. Sometimes the victims just got in the way. I thought about the guy I robbed, how he'd told the judge he thought I should get five years. I didn't give a shit about him. He was just the guy by the register. If he had made a jump for my gun, I probably would have shot him. Then what? I'd have murdered a guy, for a hundred sixty bucks and a tank of gas. I probably deserved five years. Perhaps the difference between me and Ed and Kimball was that maybe I would never go back to jail, that maybe I'd never rob anyone else, never hold a gun on another person, but those guys—they were going to do this for the rest of their lives. And what about me? I was a good kid, wasn't I? I mean, basically? Underneath it all? Once you got to know me?

I had begun to think a lot about the Grand Human Invention and about what really matters to us as humans, and it seemed books were at the center of it all. There was this discussion that stretched all the way back to the origins of human consciousness and forward into an unknowable distant future. It wasn't just in books; it was in the advancement of knowledge everywhere, the fumbling for truth that always went on with human beings. It was architecture and fashion, the evolution of cities and culture. It was wave after wave of change in everything human beings created. I began to imagine being a part of it in some way. I'd flip through the pages of my own poetry, and though most of it was clearly immature, there was obviously promise. It began to seem to me that with enough time, with enough reading, enough thought, anyone could really take part in this discussion, this advancement, this evolution.

I'd dare to imagine myself as a *real* artist, a *real* thinker. It seemed noble to me. And it seemed so possible sometimes, but other times, it seemed idiotic to even imagine myself in such a role.

— — —

And what about what I knew now, about everything, about the Invention, about life . . . ? Did it mean anything? Would it make a difference?

I was suddenly afraid. My heart began to beat fast and I felt a cold sweat come up. I had the feeling, a revolting feeling, that maybe I wasn't such a basically good kid after all. Maybe I *was* one of those people. And maybe I *would* come back.

[FORTY-FOUR]

The day I got my last in-school suspension—the in-school suspension that ultimately led to the fire and my expulsion, my night in juvie and all that—I was sitting in math class and I couldn't pay attention. The teacher's name was Mr. Hallinson. About four and a half feet tall, a bald little weasel with a whiny voice. I couldn't listen to him. His voice was driving me nuts. I couldn't sit still. I had an impulse to move around every couple of minutes, get up and walk around the class, go to the chalkboard and write something, throw an eraser at a friend. I was like a hyperactive autistic kid. This was about two weeks after I'd run out of pills. I was losing it, and I didn't know why, but of course it was because the shit was leaving my system. I was becoming dopamine and norepinephrine deficient.

I got up and walked to the board.

Hallinson intercepted me. "What do you think you're doing?"

I went around him, picked up a piece of chalk, and wrote FUCK THIS CLASS on the board.

He said, his face turning red, "Erase that right now!"

I turned and said, "You do it." I threw the eraser across the room at Rich Bass, who was laughing in the back row.

Hallinson lost his mind. He started screaming, "Get out of this class right now! Get out! Go to the office!"

— — —

Callander stared at me from his side of the desk and I slouched in my chair chewing on my lip. "What're you doing, Nate? Thought you were all better now."

"I did too," I said.

"Why don't you just drop out?" he asked.

"I can't. My parents won't let me."

"That's too bad," he said.

I got three days of in-school suspension for disrupting math class. There's a closet right off Callander's office with a desk and a chair in it. That's where you sit for three days. He gives you a list of questions, personal questions: How do your parents get along? What do you like and dislike most about school? How do you get along with your friends? You're supposed to write ten pages of answers a day. I'd had in-school suspension before and wrote only a few pages, and that turned out to be fine. I didn't want to write this time. I couldn't focus. I couldn't think.

The confines of the closet drove me insane. I walked out of there every twenty minutes and went outside to smoke. I wandered around the grounds, down to the football field, into the woods. I smoked and fretted. It was agony—the harshest, most profound frustration I'd ever felt. I leaned against the closed-up concession stand by the football field, completely disappointed in myself and the world. There just did not seem to be a way forward. I spun around and punched the wall of the concession stand. Then I held my fist and fought back the tears.

At one point during the in-school suspension, Callander brought me out of the closet into his office and said that I was being withdrawn from art class at the teacher's request.

"My God," I said. "Art is the only class that I work in. It's the only class I enjoy."

"Mrs. Indlestein says you're a disruption."

"I'm not a disruption in that class!"

"That's the way it is," he said.

This hurt. Indlestein seemed to like me. She was young and not bad-looking. I liked her. The treachery! True, she was always writing my parents. True, there was always a satanic theme to my art, but really, man— was that her place? At least I did the work!

I made it through three days of suspension. On the last day, I wrote ten pages quickly and handed them to Callander.

"What's this?" he asked.

"The questions."

He laughed. "I need thirty pages. This isn't going to cut it. And if you're in there tomorrow, it'll be forty."

My vision began to blur. I wanted to bash the motherfucker's head in right there. I turned slowly and went back into the closet, shut the door behind me, and stared at the wall. I couldn't take another day. It was already two o'clock, and there was no way in hell I could write twenty pages in two hours. I sat down and stared at the wall. I listened to that bastard go about his business. Someone was brought into his office.

I heard him say, "So what did you do this time?" Same thing he always said to me.

I heard Rich Bass's voice. "I didn't do anything. She says I was talking to Roger during class and I wasn't. I hate that kid. I wouldn't talk to him."

Callander says, "I've got to call your probation officer."

Rich says, "Come on, man! For what? I didn't do anything."

"Your PO said if you got in trouble one more time, Rich, I've got to call."

I listened for half an hour. Eventually they left and the office was quiet. I went out and got my ten pages. I was disgusted. Fucking cocksucker. I had answered those questions honestly. I told them what I thought about Dad and why I didn't like school. I talked about Joan and Philip and the rest of the kids I knew. I felt like an ass. Nobody deserved to know this stuff. I went back into my closet and started wadding up the sheets. By the time I was finished there was a pile of wadded-up sheets of paper on my desk, a little pyramid. I took my cigarette lighter out of my pocket, paused for a moment, then set the paper on fire. Up it went, and fast. I jumped up and left the room, passed quickly through the outer office where the receptionist sat. When sneaking out that week, I had been careful, moved slowly, and she'd never noticed me leave. This time she did. I walked out of the office and started down the hall, took my smokes out of my pocket, stuck one in my mouth, and lit it. Some girl who barely knew me passed by, gasped, and said, "What are you doing?"

I knew Joan was in home ec now. I went to the room, banged on the door. Mrs. Marsel opened the door. "Joan here?" I said.

She hesitated. "Yes." She disappeared.

Joan came out and I took a triumphant drag from the smoke. "What the fuck are you doing?" she said.

"Fuck this place," I said. "I did it. This is it. It's all over."

Just then Callander rounded the curve in the hallway and yelled, "Nathan!" I took off, ran out the door, and sprinted across the field. He stood at the door and yelled, "Nathan, come back here!"

"Fuck you!"

"Come back or I'll call the police!"

"Fuck you! Call the fucking pigs! I don't care!"

And with that, I disappeared into the woods.

In the woods there was an observation tower, twenty feet tall. I climbed the steps and sat at the top and smoked, thinking about what might happen. I expected the cops to come, to take me home, to tell my parents, and maybe—maybe—I'd go back to the hospital. I waited and waited, and finally got bored. So what to do?

I made my way back out of the woods and into the elementary school. This was where the art class was held—I don't know why. We were constantly walking back and forth across a country road from one building to another even though you'd think this was kind of dangerous. I walked to the art room. It was during my usual art period, so my class would be in there—just like old times. I slapped the door handle down and kicked it open.

I burst in like a mass murderer and said to Indlestein, "That's right, bitch. I'm back, and there's not a goddamned thing you can do about it."

She was stunned. I walked to my usual seat by Heidi and sat down. I told Heidi, "I set the fucking office on fire. The cops should be here anytime."

Her eyes widened. "No, you didn't."

"Yes, I did."

I noticed Indlestein whispering in the ear of a boy next to her desk. It was the retarded kid in the class, the suck-ass. He left the room. I yelled after him, "That's right, go tell them the juvenile fucking delinquent is here."

Indlestein's eyes went wide as she said, "No, no! That's not what he's doing. He's just, uh, getting some more pencils."

"Bullshit."

"I swear he's not going to tell anyone."

"Well, at least I won't have to fucking kill you, then."

She paused. She looked afraid. She asked, "Why are you doing this?"

"Because I hate this school. I hate you. I hate the administration. Why did you betray me?"

"I—I didn't betray you," she stammered.

I gave her that look. *Come on now!*

She said, "Honestly, I didn't."

I lit a smoke and watched her while I smoked. Within minutes, the door opened and Callander entered with a sheriff's deputy. The cop's name was Maize. Everybody knew him. He was a fat old guy who'd arrested everyone I knew at one time or another. They cleared the other students and Indlestein out of the room.

I said, "See you, Indlestein, you disappointment."

Maize walked over to me and said, "Put that god-damn cigarette out. This is a school. What the hell's the matter with you?"

I took one last hit, dropped it onto the floor, and ground it out beneath my boot.

"All right, let's go," he said, and we walked out the side door. On the way to the cruiser, which was parked in front of the building, he asked, "You don't have any guns or knives on you, do you?"

"No," I said. He handcuffed me and put me in the backseat. We drove back to the high school and I waited locked up in the car while everyone filled out the necessary reports. Meanwhile kids who knew me passed by the car looking in at me. I smiled at them, showed my handcuffs.

When Maize got back in the car, he said, "Well, I'm

charging you with aggravated arson. Aggravated because you could've hurt a lot of people in there." He pulled out of the school parking lot.

"So what happens now?" I asked.

"You're going to the detention center for now, and after that I don't know."

You hear rumors all your life about the JDC—juvenile detention center—and you don't like what you hear, but when a kid is sent there you suddenly have a whole new kind of respect for them. Now I was that kid. Of course I was scared, but in some way I was also proud, like I was graduating.

The JDC is a miniature prison about ten minutes north of Mercantile on Route 33. There is one central building, which houses the offices, the cafeteria, and the gymnasium. Shooting off from this building are two wings—one for the boys and one for the girls. The offices are nice: clean, well kept, modern. The cafeteria has sparkling orange plastic tables and chairs; the gymnasium has a polished wood floor and the walls are so spotless you can almost see your reflection.

The wings, on the other hand, are a different story. The group showers are unpainted cinder block covered with mold. The fixtures are rusty. The floor is slick with dirt and shit. The cells are like dungeons. They were painted once, but now they're smeared with human grease, and the windows are so dirty that barely any light gets through. The screens are caked with black film. The beds are slabs of concrete, each with a cracked plastic mattress and one blanket. The plastic scratches your skin.

One yellow lightbulb is up in a mesh cage near the ceiling in the farthest corner of the cell.

I got there during dinner. After being processed and strip-searched, I was let into the cafeteria. I walked in and looked around. What a bunch of losers. Then I heard, "Nate! Hey, Nate!" It was Rich Bass.

Callander had called Bass's PO after all. I took my tray to his table and sat down. "Dude," he said, "what the fuck are you doing here?"

"Right after you left, man, I set the office on fire."

He was impressed. Everyone was. You set your school on fire and you've instantly earned the respect of every juvenile delinquent in the state. We ate our fried chicken. Rich insisted that he hadn't done anything wrong, that he'd been set up. The other guys told us we'd get years. They said we'd be taken to court for arraignment in the morning, but neither of us would be released. I was worried. "Arson?" they said. "You're fucked, man."

After dinner we played rummy. My parents came to visit me and, alone with them in a small holding room, I broke down. They asked me why I had done it. I told them I had no idea, that I wished I hadn't, that now everything was ruined. Mom held me. They didn't say much.

Soon it was time for bed. As we entered the wing, the guards made us line up and strip down to nothing. We were each handed a pair of gym shorts before being locked in our cells. I lay on my bunk, curled up against the wall. My cellmate, a kid who had stolen a car in Detroit and made it all the way to Mercantile on his way to who knows where, talked to his partner through a screen in the wall.

I cried. I clenched my hand over my mouth and nose to keep from making noise, but I'm sure the others could hear me. I fell asleep.

Next morning our cell door was thrown open at five thirty. The guards yelled, "Get up!" We lined up in the hallway and handed in our gym shorts. Then into the shower—ten boys at a time. Freezing water, no soap. I'm disoriented. Guards yelling, "Hurry the fuck up, ladies. We don't have all day." As we exit the shower we're handed a washcloth.

We had breakfast, which wasn't bad. Scrambled eggs and bacon and white toast. After that, we played some more rummy.

Soon it was time to go to court. It was Rich and me and another kid we didn't know. The three of us sat in the back of a sheriff's deputy's cruiser, and the whole way this kid we didn't know kept saying, "Goddamn, I'm going home. You guys are fucked. Don't even think you're going home 'cause you're not. You with your fucking aggravated arson charge, and you with your probation violation. No, you guys are gonna rot in that prison. I'm getting laid tonight. Think about that."

Well, that prick was sent back to JDC and his court date was set for two months away. Rich and I were both given house arrest until our own court dates.

My mom and dad were there. So was Joan. We all went out for lunch afterward and everyone talked about the weather and whatever movies might have been coming out. I had just officially become part of the system.

— — —

My mom and I attended an informal hearing in the office of the superintendent. We'd checked out the GED program at an adult-learning center in Beckettstown and found that I could go there, get my GED, and be done with school forever. But we needed the school to sign off. We sat at a big table with Callander and the super and a couple of secretaries. The super asked me, "What do you think you'll do if we let you come back to school?"

"Exactly what I did last time," I said.

Callander stifled a laugh and shook his head.

They signed the papers, and I was officially withdrawn from high school.

[FORTY-FIVE]

Evans came to take me to the shower, and while we rode down in the elevator, he asked me how many days I had left.

"A hundred and eight days," I said.

"So is that it for you?" he asked.

"What do you mean?"

"This all the time you're ever gonna do? This one year?"

"I hope."

"Where you gonna be next year?"

"I don't know, man."

Evans said, "Look at all these fucking guys in this jail. Where do you think they'll be in a year? How about all those kids you shared a cell with? Where do you think they'll be?"

"Prison, probably."

"I see you reading all the time. You gonna go to school?"

"I think about it."

He nodded. "Do more than think about it, man. Otherwise . . ." He looked around, kind of shrugged. "You know what I mean?"

"Yeah," I said. "I do."

— — —

It wasn't long after this conversation with Evans that a bunch of guards ran past Dicky and me on our way down to rec. They all had their rubber gloves on. They lined up and rushed into a cell block.

Josh was with us. He said, "Just stand here. Hold on."

Dicky and I watched. There was yelling and screaming, scuffling, and one of the inmates was dragged out, restrained, and taken to a private cell.

Later, Josh told us somebody in the cell block had raped another inmate. They found a rag with blood and shit on it in the guy's cell.

— — —

Down in the rec yard, I said to Dicky, "You're wrong about me, man."

"What do you mean?"

"I'm fucking done with crime."

"No, you're not."

"Yes, I am."

"You'll be back here within a year. I guarantee it."

I thought about what Evans had said, and I thought

about the rag with the blood and shit on it. I thought about going to college, and I thought about writing and publishing books of my poetry, about attending poetry readings, and living on my own.

I wanted to live. I wanted to drink coffee in a Paris café. I wanted to wander the streets of New York City and have a smoke while watching the tugs float up the East River, maybe write a poem about the Brooklyn skyline.

"Bullshit," I said. "I'm gonna roam the world and write poems, fuck crazy little artist girls in Paris, smoke pot with geniuses, and become a great painter."

"You think?"

"I don't even need to be in Paris, man. I can fuck artist girls anywhere. I could probably find an artist girl in Brickville if I looked hard enough. That's not the point. The point is that the world has a hell of a lot more to it now than it did before. I had a little fucking mind before. That's not the case now. I can do anything, anywhere. That's the point. It's *possible* to live a good, rich life."

"Of course it's possible." He looked at me like I had just announced I had discovered the alphabet.

"No, you don't understand, man. A year ago I wanted my ex-girlfriend to get pregnant so that I could get a factory job and drink beer in a crappy little apartment, play my guitar a little bit, and go on that way, day in and day out, for the rest of my fucking life. For a little while, I *wanted* that. Then I wanted to die—I just wanted to kill a bunch of people first. Crime like I saw it was a roundabout form of suicide, man. I just didn't know about everything else. I didn't know about being intellectually *engaged* with life."

"Sounds to me like you didn't know much."

I glared at him. "At least I didn't kill my fucking grandmother."

"She wasn't my grandmother."

"You want me to break your nose, cocksucker?"

"Hey, whatever, man." And he grabbed the basketball and threw it as hard as he could at the wall.

[FORTY-SIX]

Joan was at my house every day while I was under house arrest. We spent a lot of time in the carport smoking and making out and talking about what the future looked like, about us getting jobs and getting married and living together.

There was one night when I suspect the Charinton-administered chemicals had completely depleted themselves from my system, or maybe it was just the shock of finding myself in this new position—kicked out of school, under house arrest, facing possible jail time in a juvenile prison—and I became quiet.

She asked me what was wrong.

"I don't know. I just feel like there's nothing left sometimes, like I'm just completely empty."

She rubbed my back and said, "They've broken your spirit."

I walked away from her, turned around, and said,

"What the fuck does that mean? They haven't fucking *broken* me!"

"I hope not," she said. "They break everyone eventually."

"Are *you* broken?" I asked.

She shrugged. "I think I've been broken for a long time."

— — —

We were sitting out in front of my house. Joan was sitting on the stoop with her guitar, practicing "Fade to Black," Metallica, and I was leaning against the fender of Dad's car, smoking, watching her.

She said, "I can't do this fucking part. You remember how it goes? Right after the beginning?"

I took the guitar from her and ran through the first part of the song.

"Right there," she said.

I slowed down. "See, it's down here, and then there." I slowly played the part and gave her the guitar back.

She played it through, then looked up at me and smiled.

"That's fucking awesome," I said.

"I love you," she said.

"I love you too."

I smiled. I did—I loved the hell out of her. I looked around. I looked up the street toward the center of town, and then back down the street toward the bridge. It all felt right. It felt perfect. I told her.

"It feels like this is the way it's always going to be."

"Do you want it to be?" she asked.

"Yeah. I do."

"Then it will be."

— — —

Later we exchanged rings, our engagement rings, and then she gave me that cheap gold necklace. I wore it every day.

She said something like, "Now our souls are bound together, for life and death." And that's what I wanted. That's what I thought she wanted too.

We were together for four months, but I can't say with any certainty that I ever knew exactly what she was thinking, what she was planning, whether what she was telling me was real or fiction.

Dad sold Joan a little Dodge Omni for five hundred bucks, but she could only give him fifty dollars down and twenty bucks a week. It was a decent little car, a standard, and she couldn't drive a standard, but she could learn. So we went out for a driving lesson. Dad was in the front with Joan; Jim and I were in the back. We lurched and ground for an hour, and by the time Dad, out of utter exasperation, declared her capable, the clutch was practically destroyed. Dad even warned her that now she'd have to buy a clutch within six months. But she got the hang of it soon enough, and we drove that Omni everywhere.

— — —

Things started going downhill, though. I could sense a distance growing. Joan had things on her mind. She started talking about her dad, about all the shit she'd been through in her life, and at first she told me some pretty horrible things. She said she hated her dad. I pressed her on it. "Why do you hate him so much?"

"Same reason I hate all the others."

"All the others, who?"

"It doesn't matter."

Then things really began to crumble, and for no apparent reason.

We were sitting out in the Omni down the street from my house when she told me she had to get away for a while. She wanted to drive out to Utah to see her dad.

"Why the fuck would you want to see your dad?" I asked. "You hate him, don't you?"

"No," she said, "he's all right."

I told her I didn't want her to go because she wouldn't come back. She promised that she'd come back. I got out and slammed the door. "Fine, fucking leave then," I said, and kicked the fender, denting it.

I walked into the house and slammed the door.

"What's wrong?" Dad asked.

"Joan's leaving. She's going to Utah."

"She's not taking that car!" he said. He ran out, ran up to the car, reached in, and snagged the keys. She still owed him hundreds of dollars, and they hadn't transferred the title. She got out and threw a fit.

"Give me the keys!" she yelled.

"Like hell!" Dad said. "I'll give you your money back, but you're not getting these fucking keys."

"That's *my* car!"

Dad turned and went toward the house.

"Kiss my ass," he said. He went inside.

I stood staring at her. I loved her. I truly loved her, and I didn't want her to leave. She started walking, and I followed, fairly far behind her. She walked all over town, down the tracks, up by the ice cream shop, past the little grocery store where I was caught stealing cigarettes the first time I tried, long before I became any good at it, uptown, past the video store, the furniture store, the post office, the pizza shop, and the bank. I followed her, never closing the distance, remaining about fifty yards behind her. I knew she would leave me, that this was the end. I cried as I followed her.

— — —

About a week later Joan said her dad was coming to visit. It was the Fourth of July and he wanted to see family in the area. I didn't see Joan much while her dad was there. On the morning he was supposed to leave, his car pulled up in front of my house. It was loaded with all of Joan's things.

On the sidewalk in front of my house, I stood facing Joan. She was crying.

She said, "I'm just going for a little while. I'll be back soon."

I said, "I doubt that."

"Why would you doubt that?"

I shrugged.

She hugged me and got my neck wet with tears. Then she backed off.

"I love you," she said.

"I love you too."

She got into the car, and they drove away.

I think I was in some kind of shock. I didn't feel any-thing that day.

[FORTY-SEVEN]

Sentencing day in Paradise County Superior Court. When I walked into the courtroom with Kline, my mom stood and came over to us. She told Kline, "I'm going to hug my son."

"I'm sorry, ma'am. I can't let you touch him."

She ignored him, put her arms around me, and held me. I wanted to cry. My dad and brother were seated near the front. They waved.

My public defender and the prosecutor had already worked out a plea bargain. If the judge accepted it, I'd get a year, basically, and since I had already served nine months, I'd be out in three months. My public defender had warned me that he might not accept it, and that he might very well send me to prison. Even if he accepted the plea bargain, I'd still have three months left to serve, and I could still go to prison for those three months.

There was a possibility that I could stay in the county jail, but it wasn't guaranteed.

The victim, the guy at the truck stop who worked the register, sat in the front row. He glared at me. At one point the prosecutor asked him what kind of sentence he thought I should get. He said, "Five straight years."

When the judge heard this, he said, "You know, I have a daughter who's going to school up north. Last spring I bought her a new car, and just a few months ago it was broken into. The window was smashed, the stereo was stolen, and I'll tell you, if the perpetrators of that crime were to come before me, I would no doubt want to sentence them to twenty years of hard labor. But that's not right. I'm angry and I'm hurt because the victim was a family member and the property damaged was something I myself purchased. Now, I've gone over to that jailhouse and I've had them lock me into a cell just to see what it was like. Those cells are about six by nine feet, and when you sit down on the bunk all you see is that wall staring right at you and nothing else. It's not a pleasant experience."

My God, I thought. This might go okay.

The judge went on. "Mr. Henry has spent the last nine months in such a cell, and because he's not yet eighteen, he's basically spent the last nine months in solitary confinement—he hasn't had a television to watch like the other inmates, and except for brief periods of time, he hasn't had any cellmates. So you can imagine how it is not to have any human contact for such a long time."

Jesus, the man's actually human. He's a fucking genius.

"I'm going to accept the plea agreement reached by Mr. Henry's attorney and the prosecutor. I'm sentencing him to eight years, with six of that suspended—to be served as probation. Here in the state of Illinois if an inmate serves what is called good time, meaning if he has not been the cause of any disruptions and hasn't possessed any contraband, he's released after serving at least half of his sentence."

Three more months . . . that's enough time to still send me to prison.

"Mr. Henry has been an exemplary inmate, has caused no problems for the guards, and so I will suggest that for the remainder of his time he remain at the Paradise County Jail."

My God, it was like winning the lottery. I looked at my family. My dad smiled and my mom beamed. I looked at the judge. I couldn't believe it.

"Thank you," I said.

Kline rushed me past my mom so she wouldn't have a chance to hug me again, but that was okay. In Illinois, you serve only half your time if you haven't gotten into any trouble in jail, and I had already served nine months. I'd be home in three months, and that was all that mattered.

[FORTY-EIGHT]

After the Fourth of July, after Joan left with her dad, everything got quiet. David went to southern Indiana to visit his grandparents, and Gladine decided that I was no longer such a great influence on Philip, so our contact was limited. It was awful, being isolated from Philip, stuck in town after a lifetime of fucking around on the farm. I missed him, but at least I could still visit on the weekends. The days got longer, and things moved slower, and I was not getting letters from Joan.

I got a job at a welding shop.

I got up at seven thirty in the morning and took a shower, got dressed, watched television for a few minutes, and smoked a cigarette on the back porch. Then I rode my bike out to the welding shop, a small sheet-metal warehouse next to a cornfield less than a mile outside of town, and clocked in. I used sharp little tools to take the burrs off pieces of steel. I cut myself and bled.

I bandaged myself up and went back to work. At noon, I rode my bike back into town and had lunch with Dad, which was nice actually—we started getting along fairly well—then I rode back out to the factory.

They were teaching me how to weld. Someday, I'd be a welder. I'd wear one of those cool visors and make sparks fly all over the place, and while I was working no one would approach me or look directly at what I was doing for fear of being blinded forever. I either cleaned the burrs off the steel, wiped down big steel structures with some kind of chemical that made me nauseous, or swept the floor.

At five in the afternoon, I rode my bike home and had dinner with my parents. One of our staple meals was fish sticks, baked beans, and fried potatoes. An uncle of mine came over in the evenings to tutor me—I had no math skills. My GED test was approaching. I tried to call Joan sometimes—no one answered. I left messages. I told her I loved her. I was worried and I had no way of finding out if she was even still alive.

Finally, she called.

I took the cordless phone out into the garage—and Joan accused me of fucking around on her. I was suddenly certain that she had hooked up with somebody else, that this was her way of ending our thing without taking any responsibility. I punched the wall. I yelled into the phone, "WHAT are you doing? WHY are you doing this?"

"You know why."

"I can't believe you're doing this."

She hung up. And that was it. That was the last time I talked to her.

— — —

Philip and I were out in a field, on a hill looking north. We were drinking a couple of beers we'd stolen from Philip's dad. It felt like the end of the world. Joan was gone. David was never around anymore. I was not in school, and I hated my job. Everything was different.

"Philip, I look around at all these fucking slaves and wonder how they do it."

"I don't know, man."

"Not us."

"That's right," he said. "Not us."

"We're true anarchists, man. No rules, no laws."

Philip took another swig from his beer, nodded.

"We're beyond everything."

We were silent for a long time. I lit a smoke and drained the rest of my beer, tossed the can. Then I yelled, as loud as I could, "FUCK YOU, AMERICA!"

We went down to the road, and as we were walking back to Philip's house, a nice-looking Honda stopped beside us. It was Justin O'Reilly.

"What are you guys up to?" he asked.

Ever since he broke my nose, we got along all right. Though as far as I was concerned, Justin and I had always gotten along. It was Norton I wanted to decapitate with a chainsaw.

"Nothing." I leaned against the car. "Just talking about getting the fuck outta here."

"Oh, yeah?" His stereo had been on, kind of low, but he turned it off.

Philip said, "Going to Canada, fuck us some Canadian bitches." He laughed. "Kill some motherfuckers on the way."

"Shut up, Philip," Justin said and looked at me. "Canada, huh?"

I shrugged. "You want to go?"

"Nah." He smiled. "Somebody's got to stick around to keep Norton out of prison."

"I heard that," I said.

Then Justin waved and drove off. We started walking again.

Philip said, "You should blow Norton's head off before we go."

"Maybe." I nodded. "I'd like to."

[FORTY-NINE]

I stretched the phone cord across my cell and sat down on my bunk.

"David's working on a farm now," Philip said.

"Yeah, doing what?"

"Shoveling shit, castrating pigs. All that disgusting shit they do on farms."

"How much is he getting paid?" I really didn't care. I just didn't know what else to say.

"Six bucks an hour."

"Not bad." I took a sip of my coffee and heard the jingle of a guard's keys. It was about time for the crazies to go to rec.

"Is Joan still around?" I asked.

"I think she went back to Utah."

"Really?" I felt immense relief.

"Yeah. Probably never see that bitch again."

"I hope not." I got up and grabbed my window

blind—the folded sheet of paper—from under my bunk and stuffed it against the cell door's window.

"I talked to Amy the other day," he said. "She said to tell you hi."

I stopped in the center of the cell. "Amy? How's she doing?"

"Okay, I guess."

I sat back down on my bunk. The crazies were passing my door. One of them kicked it. "Get the fuck out of here!" I yelled. Then I was quiet for a minute. I said, "She still in Colorado?"

"Yeah."

I took the blind down from my window.

Philip said, "I've got to go do this scared-straight shit at the prison next week."

"Might be interesting," I said.

"Fucking sucks. A year probation, community service, this scared-straight shit."

"Sounds like cake, man."

"Cake, my ass."

"You got off easy."

"Easy? Are you nuts?"

"You're complaining? I've been sitting in here for a fucking year, and you're complaining?"

There was a silence that seemed uncomfortable, so I told him I had to go.

"All right," he said. "How many days left?"

"Twenty-eight."

"Well, I'll see you in twenty-eight days then."

"All right, man." And I hung up.

[FIFTY]

One day when I came home from the welding shop for lunch, Dad had ordered food for us from the diner across the street, the same thing he had always gotten there: two fish deluxe sandwiches with fries.

"You're doing real good, Nate," Dad said. "You really put us through hell for the last couple years."

"Yeah, I know."

"But now you're a working man." He smiled.

"Yup." I gave a fake grunt. "I am a working man."

"Getting your GED, working every day."

"Yeah."

"Now it don't seem so much like you're gonna end up dead."

I looked at him. I didn't know what to say.

"'Cause that's what it looked like for a long time. We expected it."

We ate in silence for a while; then he said, "You know, I died all those times and was brought back to life—I always thought there was a reason for it, like I was meant to do something important."

I bit into my fish deluxe.

"I never did anything important," he said, "but I hope you do. You understand me?"

"Yeah, I think so."

"So, you're doing good. I mean it."

"Thanks, Dad."

— — —

Next day I'm grinding down the rough-cut edges of a piece of steel with an electric grinder, and I look up and around at all the other guys in the shop who are engaged in similar types of work. I look out the open bay doors of the warehouse, and there's the bright sun and open fields and I think, "Is this it? Is this my life?" And I think of the whole Canada fantasy Philip and I always talked about. Canada. What the fuck? Get up there to some other town, maybe some town on the East Coast, a fishing town, and get a job like this, only I'm not cutting burrs off steel, I'm gutting fish all day long. Hardly worth the trouble. This is death, I thought. This is infinite misery, infinite nothingness. Then I thought of Joan. Maybe this bullshit would've been worth it if I still had her. The bullshit *was* worth it when she was here. Life seemed to mean something.

My chest seized and my facial muscles clenched. It

was a good thing I wore a visor. What if these assholes saw me crying? Imagine that.

— — —

"Is Philip there?" I jumped up and sat on the welding table, lit up a cigarette. I had ten minutes. "Hey, what's up? Philip, we're changing plans. I want to go to LA, and on the way we're stopping in Salt Lake City to put a bullet in Joan's fucking head."

"Really?" He wasn't completely surprised.

"Really. That's what I want to do."

"Okay. Cool."

I had the necklace, the cheap fourteen-karat gold necklace Joan had given me at the beginning of our relationship, and on this necklace I had both our engagement rings. I can't remember why I had hers as well—seems like she should've taken it with her when she left. I would take this necklace and hang it over the door handle on the front door of her trailer, when we got to Salt Lake City, and when she came outside and found that necklace, she'd know that I'd come—and not come to plead for her love or to ask for her forgiveness. She'd get no tears from me.

I loved a movie called *Wisdom*. It stars Emilio Estevez in the lead role, Demi Moore as his girlfriend. John Wisdom has a car-theft conviction on his record from when he got drunk on prom night and went for a drunken joy ride—wrecked the car. So since this conviction is on his record, he can't get a real job and ends up in a fast-food joint, self-esteem shot, hating life. He decides to become a criminal (since, he reasons, that's how society already sees him) but can't decide what crime he wants to do. He runs over the list—kidnapping, robbery, murder. Nothing sounds good to him. He buys an Uzi and a big military jacket under which he can hide it, and sort of wanders around waiting for the crime to come to him. Middle of the night, sitting in a bus station, watching a little pay TV, a news story about all these banks foreclosing on all these poor farmers, taking their farms and land away from them, tossing them out on the street—poor, miserable bastards—and suddenly Wisdom gets an idea. He would drive across the country blowing up bank documents. He'd go into these banks and whip out his machine gun, just like he was going to rob the place, but instead he'd just toss dynamite at their filing cabinets. Now, you can imagine that I thought this mission of his was pretty weak, though I loved the whole idea—machine guns, banks. He ends up killing a cop and his girlfriend gets shot; then he himself is shot dead by a few dozen FBI agents. Man, I thought, what a way to go.

So I said to Philip, "Tonight's the night. All the way to California, Wisdom-style. That's what I'm talking about. Get the pistol, get all your shit together, and meet me at the covered bridge at twelve forty-five . . . Yeah, *a.m.* I'll be in my mom's car—when I get to the stop sign, I'll flip the headlights off and then back on. That way you'll know it's me. All right? You okay with this? Good. Be cool, man."

I hopped down from the table and went back to work for the rest of the day.

[FIFTY-ONE]

It was the middle of the night and the jail was dead silent. I put down my book and looked at my watch. It was four thirty. Mom would be getting up for work soon, just like she did every morning. She'd been getting up at four thirty every morning for something like fifteen years. She gets out of bed, turns the radio on in the kitchen, makes her morning cup of tea, and drinks it before she gets in the shower. What does she think about? How does she do it day after day? I asked her once, didn't she hate work? She said of course. But if she thought about that, she wouldn't be able to do it. So every morning, whether she's slept well or not, whether she has a migraine or not—and she does get migraines; I've seen her cry because of her migraines—she gets up and goes to work.

She worked in a factory, assembled thermostats. It was a repetitive job. She placed washers onto rods that attached to valves. They used to have family day at her job, and I went there a couple of times to see where she spent her days. The factory was a string of silver-arched buildings, like airplane hangars. It was hot in there, and noisy. There were windows high up, which were open, but it was still hard to breathe. It was an awful place.

Mom got her job there not long after she married Dad. She must have learned early that if she didn't keep the family afloat financially, no one would. Dad said working made him sick, physically sick, and he'd sleep for days. He didn't want Mom to go to work either, so he'd sometimes sabotage the car, remove the plug wires, so that she'd have to stay home. She was suspended once for attendance, I think, because of this.

Mom once told me she'd had plans to go to college, but those plans fell apart because she had to work. Dad never held a job for very long. There was a time when he did have a job for a while, as the maintenance man at a small office building near downtown Indianapolis. He had that job for two years. For those two years, the money seemed to roll in. Mom was happy, Dad was happy—we did things. We went on vacation; we got a camper and went to campgrounds. We got a new car, Dad got a new motorcycle, a credit card came in the mail. We were practically middle class. Then Dad lost the job, or quit, and the car and the bike were repossessed, the credit card became another debt, and the camper languished in the backyard.

But Mom always did what she thought she had to do. She went to work every day. She made sure we had food, she paid the bills; every year we had new school clothes and supplies, we had good Christmases. And this was all because of her. Now she had a son in jail for armed robbery, and it was killing her.

Sitting in jail, thinking about my mom at four thirty in the morning, I felt sick to my stomach. I felt like I wanted to vomit. I felt like I was shit, like I had done nothing but contribute to how difficult my mom's life was. She should've left Dad, I thought, maybe married some reasonable man, and things could have been different. But maybe Dad had nothing to do with anything. He was, in a weird way, always there for me, and he loved me, and the more I thought about it, the more it became clear he wasn't some kind of crazed loser who sat around the house all the time doing nothing. The man turned a shitty, run-down house into what felt like a middle-class dwelling. New floors in the kitchen and bathroom, new walls, new fixtures. He remodeled the entire interior of the house. He kept the roofs from leaking, kept the cars running, built the carport and the garage and storage buildings with his own hands. In the winter when the pipes would freeze, he'd get on his overalls and climb down into the icy crawl spaces with a blowtorch and thaw out the pipes—it would take hours down there in the cold. He did what he had to do too, I suppose. They both did.

Maybe I couldn't blame any of this on anyone.

Maybe it was all me. I was fucked up. Just completely fucked up, all the way to the core. Maybe it was so deep there was nothing anyone could do about it. The horror of this got into my stomach and twisted heavily.

[FIFTY-TWO]

Jim told me on the phone what happened at home that night after I left—the night the robbery happened. After getting dressed and gathering my supplies, I wrote a note for my parents, telling them that I wasn't cut out for a life of nine to five, that I had to be free, even if it meant that I had to die. I told them it had nothing to do with them, that they had been fine parents, and that I had enjoyed spending my lunches with Dad for the past couple of weeks. I told them I loved them, but that greater things awaited me.

Mom had left me a note on the dining room table, like she did almost every night. I read it. "Have a good day, honey. I love you." I wrote underneath her writing, "I love you too." Then I left.

Apparently not long after I left, she got up to go to the bathroom and noticed my handwriting on her note. She read the note I'd left them, and woke Dad up. Dad checked his guns, found one missing, went outside, and saw the car was gone. He went across the street to a neighbor's house, a guy he talked to sometimes, and showed him the note. Dad didn't know what to do. The guy asked him if he had called the cops, and Dad said not yet. He went home and called the cops, then called Gladine, asked her if Philip was still there. She went up and checked, came back to the phone, and said he was. Dad told her to check again.

Philip had rolled blankets up under his sheet to make it look like he was still there. She came back to the phone, said he was gone. Gladine got dressed and drove to my parents' house. The deputy sheriff came and made a report. Then they waited.

A few hours later the Paradise County sheriff's department called Mom and Dad. Their car had been used in a robbery in Illinois. About an hour after that, they called again, said a high-speed chase was under way outside a town called Burroughstown. They called back later and said we'd been arrested, and that they'd better come.

So they drove to Illinois.

What a nightmare.

— — —

I had two hundred dollars in the bank in Brickville but, amazingly, I forgot to withdraw it. Two hundred dollars might have gotten us legally all the way to Utah—wouldn't have had to rob anyplace until after the murder. Besides, I was beginning to think maybe executing Joan wasn't such a good idea. When I told Philip, a little north of Dayton, that I might not kill her, he asked if we could stop anyway, if I minded if he fucked her.

"Yes, I mind. Jesus . . ."

"Just asking, dude."

Interstate 70 heading west for hours, forever, it felt like, and by the time we crossed the state line, we were almost out of gas and the engine was overheating. It had to be soon. Philip kept falling asleep and I woke him up again and again, asked him how the fuck he could sleep on the most important night of our lives. He said he had to piss. He either slept or pissed all night long. We walked into a rest area and he asked me if I had my piece, and I said of course. "Do you? Go get your fucking gun, man. Keep that thing with you at all times, dude. This is not a goddamn road trip to the Grand Canyon—we're not on a fucking weekend vacation. Go get the fucking gun. I'll wait here for you, keep an eye out."

In the harsh fluorescent light, Philip was pale, his eyes were red, and he looked like a little boy. He was fourteen years old and he thought I was going to take care of him.

"Man, it's like a dream," I told him. "I could slaughter a whole family right now and not feel a thing."

We crossed the state line into Illinois.

We pulled into a gas station and parked. The engine was too hot to go on. It was about three thirty in the morning and the place was dead. There was one guy inside, behind the register reading a magazine and smoking a cigarette. I went in and asked him if I could get some water for the radiator. He found me a bucket, showed me where the spout was out behind the building, even filled the bucket himself and carried it out to the front for me. Philip popped the hood and we opened the radiator. It was empty. The guy went back into the shop, back to his magazine; Philip and I went around to the rear of the car and leaned against the trunk, lit up cigarettes. Philip asked if this was the place.

"No, man. This guy's way too cool."

"Where, then?"

I pointed to a place directly across the street—one of those giant truck stops, a mega truck stop, one with a full-size restaurant and oversize fueling area, practically a mall inside—but it was dead. There were no customers. The place was all lit up, but it looked like a ghost town.

"You pump the gas," I said. "And I'll go inside, use the john. When you're finished pumping, get back in the car, start it up, and slide back over into the passenger seat. Be real careful with the gas pedal—it's touchy. If you flood the thing out, we're fucked."

"Okay."

— — —

As I swung the door open and pocketed the .25 auto that I'd stolen from Dad—he must have hidden his .380; I couldn't find it anywhere—Philip assured me that he had my back. "Anything goes wrong and I'll open fire on the motherfuckers."

I said all right and headed for the door. It was a long walk from where the car was parked to the front door.

I walked, strutted, looking around lazily like I was minding my own business. Looked back and Philip was already pumping gas.

Hit the door and nodded to the guy behind the counter, noticed another guy crouched on the floor by the counter talking to him. This guy wore all white, a cook or dishwasher—I nodded to him too and headed for the restroom. Stood at the urinal and pretended to piss. I wore a navy blue trench coat with holes cut into the pockets—I slid the gun through the hole for practice. Smooth. Put the gun away and moved to the sink, turned on the cold water, looked at my bad self in the mirror. I was never so calm, never so in control as I was right then. Turned the water off, cracked my neck, smiled at that stone-cold hard-ass motherfucker looking back at me and headed out to do some business.

"Don't take this personal, man," I said. "It's got nothing to do with you. I just need the money."

The dishwasher was gone now, had gone back to the kitchen or out back to smoke a joint or whatever.

I said, "I don't want to hurt anybody," and as I said this, I gripped the top portion of the automatic, slid it back and chambered a shell.

The guy asked me if I wanted the checks too.

"Nope." I grabbed the stack of cash from his hand and backed out of the store, gun level with his chest. Ran to the car, jumped in, tossed the cash and the pistol at

Philip—Philip whooped like he was out of his goddamn mind—and we drove away like the Billy the Kid, James Gang, Wisdom-style dumbasses we were—hadn't even thought about wearing masks, hadn't even thought about concealing the license plate—and when we got back out on the freeway, the engine was still hot.

[FIFTY-THREE]

I had a little over one week to go and I was beginning to feel it. For so long I had pushed away thoughts of home that now, when they began to crowd back in on me, it was as if I were imagining a mystical world coming back out of the mist and fog of the ancient past, revived, vivid, shimmering with promise. I called Mom every day now.

"I've got your room vacuumed and dusted," she said. "Your blankets and sheets are all washed and ready for you."

"I can't wait," I said. "I feel like I'm going to blow up. Every day it gets worse and worse. I can't sleep."

"Well, you got to get your sleep."

"I know."

"What do you want to do after we pick you up?"

"Go to McDonalds, get a bacon, egg, and cheese biscuit. Oh, my *God*! Just the thought of it blows my mind."

"Well, I think we can manage that."

"You know, I think I'm different now, Mom."

She was silent for a moment. "How so?" she asked.

"I don't know really. I just feel different. I feel like I'm able to appreciate things more."

"Like what?"

"I don't know . . . everything."

She didn't say anything.

"I'm sorry, Mom."

"I know, honey. I know you are."

"I don't want to keep doing this."

"I know."

[FIFTY-FOUR]

It was a hot night, August, three thirty in the morning. The engine was still hot and the getaway car was stuck at forty miles an hour.

"We can't drive like this on the freeway, man. They'll get us for sure." I pulled off at the next exit, wound away from the freeway on one-lane dirt roads that cut between cornfields. The corn was five to seven feet tall. We had to find a spot to stop and let the car cool down. Philip had to piss. We drove and drove, slowly—dead silence except for the knocking engine of the Dodge.

I couldn't find a decent pull-off, so I stopped the car in the middle of one of those roads and cut the engine, killed the lights. There was a farmhouse about a mile away—I could see the lights from where we were—but aside from that there was nothing. Philip jumped out and ran down into the ditch to piss. I leaned against the hood, counted the money—a hundred and sixty-three dollars—not much, but more than either of us had ever had at one time. I set the bills on the hood and put the gun on top of them, lit a cigarette.

"Philip, this is what all those guys must have felt, all those bank robbers and outlaws—like we crossed some line, like we're on the outside of everything now."

Philip nodded. "Fucking crazy, man." He held the small stack of bills, not counting them but shuffling them again and again. He said, "I can't believe we just fucking did that, man! We're badasses, dude!"

I didn't know how far we'd gotten away from the freeway. All those roads looked the same. Dirt roads, cornfields, little patches of trees every once in a while. There was no other span of time so pure, when so many of my concerns had been eliminated, when I was so alive, as during that hour or so directly after the robbery.

We sat on the hood and smoked for half an hour. Philip was elated, the happiest I'd ever seen him. He talked about California—didn't know what he was talking about since neither of us had ever been there, but he said, "They're gonna dig us in California, man."

"Why's that?" I asked.

"Because we're badasses. They're all badasses out there."

I didn't say much. We'd just entered the peak of this trip, and a hundred and sixty-three dollars would not get us all the way to the West Coast—there would have to be more robberies, and things might get a lot worse. The plan all along had been that if we were stopped by a cop, the cop would be shot, and this would be the last trip either of us would ever take. As far as I was concerned, we'd probably never make it to California. I imagined us ending up like that scene in *Bonnie and Clyde* when they're finally ambushed, blown to pieces by those cops with machine guns. Philip, I think, didn't understand this aspect of the journey, that it might not have a happy ending. And it didn't take long for my suspicions to be confirmed.

After the engine had cooled and it was time to get back on the road, we started off in the direction we thought the freeway was. We entered a small city called Burroughstown at about four thirty in the morning.

"What the fuck is this place? We didn't come through here before."

"I don't know."

Little redneck town. Customary grain elevators. The whole town was asleep—we were the only car on the road.

We came to a stoplight.

"Oh, fuck," Philip said. "Oh, fuck, oh, fuck." And I saw right away what he was *oh, fuck*ing about. We came to the intersection from the north. On the southwest corner there was a grocery store, and in the parking lot, facing the intersection, was a police cruiser, parking lights on.

Philip said, "What the fuck are we gonna do, man?"

I said, "We're gonna be real cool about this. Just calm down."

Our light changed to green and we pulled forward, slow and easy. The cop pulled out behind us, began to follow at a distance of about thirty feet. Exactly twenty-five miles per hour, we crawled along. I made a left turn, the cop made a left turn. All of Philip's blood had collected in his feet, and he looked like he was about to pass out.

"Oh, my God, man," he said. "I don't want to die! I don't want to die!"

Burroughstown was larger than I had thought. After a few minutes, there were three more cruisers following along behind us. Still at exactly twenty-five miles an hour, we were catching all green lights and this silent caravan kept moving. I told Philip to calm down. He was mumbling now.

He looked back. "Oh, God," he said again—more like yelped it. "There's two more cops back there."

I looked in the rearview and, sure enough, there were now six cruisers, one behind the other. My gun had been on the seat between us, so I picked it up, checked the chamber to make sure it was ready to go, and held it in my right hand, in my lap.

"I don't want to die," Philip said again, his voice weak. He had to force the words out.

"You're not gonna fucking die, man. Pick up your gun." He seemed to shrink into the seat as if all the juice had gone out of him, as if his muscles had stopped functioning. "Philip, get your fucking self together."

When there were seven police cruisers in single file, all moving along behind our little maroon Dodge Aries, probably the entire Burroughstown police force, they finally decided to act. The instant their lights came on, I hit the gas. The roar of the powerful engines in the police cars filled the air. I jammed the gas pedal into the floor, and within seconds this absurd snake of vehicles, its whole body a mess of spinning lights, was shooting down the city street at ninety miles per hour.

Philip was in a frenzy, spewing terrified gibberish into the dashboard. The gun was still in my right hand, both of my hands on the wheel. I was on the edge of the seat, hunched up over the wheel. I was screaming— screaming at Philip to get his fucking gun out.

A cruiser tried to move up beside us, I swerved toward him, and he fell back. Red and blue lights were everywhere, bouncing off the houses that lined the street. Everything was a blur—we were running red lights, we were all over the road.

Ninety-five miles per hour.

A pickup truck pulled out in front of us at an intersection and just in time jumped the sidewalk to avoid the ugliest nine-car pileup Burroughstown would have ever seen.

When we left the town behind, I could see that on almost every road connecting to the one we were on, there were blue and red lights moving in our direction. They were coming from everywhere. They were converging on us from every direction, and far ahead there were more coming toward us.

"Philip, pick up your fucking gun and be a man, you fucker!"

He had his mom's little pearl-handled .22 pistol in his two open hands on his lap, and he was looking down at it with horror, yelling, "I don't want to die, Nate!"

"Fuck these bastards, Philip!" And as we passed the mouth of a little road where another cop sat, ready to pull out and join the caravan, I aimed the gun at him, about to shoot the cop, but we passed too quickly to squeeze off a round. Or maybe just for an instant, I was reasonable enough not to—Jesus, imagine if I had . . .

"Fuck! They're everywhere!" Philip screamed. The one coming toward us was getting closer and closer.

"Hold on, man, we gotta get off this road." I hit the brakes and cut the wheel to the right and the Dodge shot off the road, through a ditch, and into a cornfield. When the car came to a stop, fifty feet into the field and the engine dead, we jumped out simultaneously and ran off into the corn.

[FIFTY-FIVE]

They finally moved me back to P-13 about a week before my release. Timmon was still next door, and on the other side of him, in P-11, was Dicky the Grandma Slayer. Those poor bastards. In one of my books I'd read the term "signifying." That's when a prisoner is getting out soon and starts to signify this, whether verbally or through his general behavior (like not concealing his excitement), to those around him. To those who aren't getting out, it can be quite upsetting. Well, I was a shameless signifier.

"Timmon!"

"What the fuck you want?"

"Six days, motherfucker!"

He and Dicky both yell, "Shut the fuck up!" And I laugh my ass off.

"Six days, bitches, and I'm smoking cigarettes, and eatin' pussy, gettin' fucking laid, chowing on whatever goddamned food I wanna eat. Did I mention pussy? Did I mention that? I don't want to forget that."

Day and night I went on this way.

"Hey, Dicky! Dicky!"

"Nate, please . . ."

"FIVE DAYS, MOTHERFUCKER! HAHA-HAHA!"

— — —

On my last night in jail, I couldn't sleep. I could barely believe I was getting out. Three hundred sixty days and I was walking out tomorrow. I paced. I tried to read, couldn't, paced, harassed Dicky and Timmon, paced. I couldn't contain myself.

At one point Josh and Kline, two of the guards I was closest to, ran into my cell suddenly and attacked me, literally, and wrestled me to the floor.

"Butt fuck him!" Josh yelled.

I screamed my head off.

Kline yelled, "He's resisting, he's resisting! File charges, quick!"

"Fuck him and then charge him!"

Then they calmed down, punched me on the shoulder, shook my hand, and said if I ever came back, they were definitely going to butt fuck me.

I said okay.

Josh smiled. "Good luck," he said. "I mean it."

"I know. Thanks."

Later I asked Dennis if I could hang out with Dicky for a while, play some cards, just to pass the time. So he took me down to Dicky's cell, and we played rummy until the sun came up.

Then I packed all my shit up in garbage bags. Leonard took me down for a shower, got the clothes I was arrested in out of the locker where they'd been stored for a year. They stuck me in P-1, to wait until eight o'clock.

— — —

I was sitting on the bunk in P-1 with three hours to go. P-1, where it had all started. I remembered that cocksucker Arnold, wondered how he was faring in the big house, whether he'd been shanked or not. Probably.

My cell door opened and Evans came in. He sat down on the other bunk.

"So, what's it gonna be, man?" he said. "Gonna see you come back here?"

"I hope not."

"What, you think you got no control?"

"Sometimes I feel like I don't," I said. I got up and leaned against the sink. "You know, man, sometimes I really feel like I can't trust myself."

He shrugged. "Just keep doing the right thing."

"I've done the right thing before. Then I did the wrong thing."

"It can always be different."

We were quiet for a while. Then I said, looking at the floor, "I'm afraid of myself, man."

He looked up at me and nodded.

"I'm really afraid of myself. I don't know who the fuck I am half the time. I mean, I don't know why I've done the things I've done. I don't feel like I can just, you know, *determine* to save myself from destruction. I feel like it's already arranged that I'm going to blow everything up. I feel like I'll do the right thing, get everything in order, start school, get a job, maybe get my own place, and then suddenly one night I'll just go out and rob some place and have no idea really why I did it. I'll be sitting back in jail, wondering how it happened. I can't trust myself. I can't believe in the future, you know?"

"I think so." Evans smoothed his mustache out with his forefinger and thumb, and nodded. "That's just a feeling. It's not real, man. It doesn't have to happen that way."

"I know. But essentially, I don't know what I am. I know what I *want* to be. I think I do. But I see all these guys who've just got nothing, man—I mean *nothing*. They don't seem to want anything beautiful or important. I don't know, maybe they do. They just don't know how to get it."

Evans nodded.

"There's a whole fucking world out there, full of languages and philosophy and cultures older than I can imagine. I want to know all this. I want to read everything. And I want to *write*, man! You realize that? I want to think, I want to *know*. The thought that I might just be doomed makes me sick to my stomach, man. I know what I've done, what I thought, what I wanted, and it all makes sense. It all had to lead here. But now what? Look at everything that has to change in order for it all to lead somewhere else."

He got up and came over to me. "You're in charge," he said, then slapped me on the shoulder. "It's up to you."

"I hope so."

"Good luck," he said, and we shook hands.

He opened the door, looked back at me, and sort of half-smiled. Then he walked out, locked the door, and went down the hall.

I thought about the Invention again. I thought about Nietzsche, Kerouac, French girls, Paris streets, or strolling some Far Eastern city with a notebook in my pocket. I thought about gallery openings and philosophical arguments, and I imagined publishing a book about everything I've seen and thought, whatever the fuck that would look like—I could barely even formulate an image of that. And then I thought about coming back to the Paradise County Jail . . .

[FIFTY-SIX]

About an hour after the sun had come up that Wednesday morning, Philip and I had been belly-crawling through corn and soybean fields for five hours. We were completely soaked, caked in mud from head to foot, exhausted. We had decided to get rid of the guns. Neither of us was any longer in the mood to engage in a gunfight with the cops, although the truth is Philip never had any interest in the shoot-out—it was my idea.

So we hid the guns in the tall grass and moved toward the freeway. We were ready to be arrested now. I assumed that because I was still on probation in Indiana, we would both be transported back to the JDC, where all the other juvenile inmates would surely regard us as absolute badasses, just like when I landed there for arson. I pictured myself there in the dayroom, Philip and I recounting our night run to a hundred rapt and adoring fans. Eat fried chicken. Play basketball. Cool off.

I was wrong.

While we halfheartedly attempted to hitchhike along Interstate 70, a cop spotted us, and instantly the police helicopter—which had been circling the field since dawn—was above us. We got away from the freeway, jumped a fence, and entered a wooded area, but I'm sure there was a sharpshooter in that chopper. We were beaded the entire time.

Moments later, the SWAT guys with assault 12-gauges, 9-millimeters, and dogs entered the woods in their black masks. Philip and I hid behind a large tree as they moved toward us.

I yelled, "We're coming out!"

We peeked around the tree. Our hands were up. In the confusion of that moment—those guns on us, the dogs barking, the helicopter just overhead—the cops were yelling at us, "Drop to the ground!" and "Where the fuck are the guns?" Then one of the dogs was let loose. It went for my balls, and had I not jerked my hips just in time, I would not be in possession of my testicles any longer. The German shepherd sank its huge fangs into my upper thigh. It tugged and twisted. It was the worst physical pain I've ever felt.

Then I was down, the barrel of a 9-millimeter shoved painfully into the back of my head, the dog gnawing on me for—I am not kidding—at least another three or four minutes.

When we were eventually led out of that little patch of woods somewhere in the middle of Illinois in handcuffs, I saw so many cruisers and emergency vehicles that I really expected to see a news crew. Rabid dogs and agitated cops aside, this was, I have to admit, quite a glorious moment—except, there were no cameras.

What a disappointment. No audience. Just cops.

[FIFTY-SEVEN]

It was eight o'clock in the morning, August 19, when I limped through Sallyport with my hands behind my back. Three hundred and sixty days ago.

Leonard squeezed a button on the CB radio on his shoulder, "Sallyport, open up." Eight o'clock in the morning, one year later (with jail sentences they go by thirty-day months). I was dressed in the exact same clothes I had been arrested in, still covered with hardened mud, holes in the thigh from where the dog had bitten me, stiff with dried blood. My black leather boots had turned gray and cracked. I had a garbage bag in my right hand, full of notebooks and sweatpants and T-shirts.

Leonard pushed the door open and held it for me. I stepped out into a garage—it smelled of oil and gasoline.

"You got a smoke, Leonard?"

He took a pack of Marlboros out of the chest pocket of his uniform and shook one out for me. I set the garbage bag down and rooted around inside until I found a manila envelope with my name on it. I opened it and took out a plastic lighter. I lit the cigarette, and Leonard said into his radio, "Open gate."

The garage door slowly rose, and beyond it, simultaneously, a ten-foot chain-link gate topped with razor wire, just like the rest of the fence that surrounds the place, automatically swung open. He patted me on the shoulder and gave me an awkward smile.

I walked out into the world and the sun burned my eyes—they teared up and I wiped at them with the back of my left hand. When the cigarette smoke got into my eyes, I realized it had been a whole year since that had happened—so it hurt like hell. I dropped the garbage bag and clutched my face with both hands. While I struggled with this pain, I felt my mom's arms around me. She hugged me.

When I looked up, Dad gave me a nod.

"Hey," I said.

Mom went on hugging me silently.

"Well, you're finally out of the clink," Dad said. "You ready to go rob another place?"

Mom turned and hit him in the ribs. "Stop it, Hank!"

We got in the car and Dad did a U-turn in the street. We drove away, and I looked back at the jail. This was really the first time I saw it from a distance. It was just a squat brick rectangle with narrow windows and a fence around it. It looked small. It looked like any other building.

"Back to Brickville," Dad said.

"Yeah," I said. "Back to Brickville."

[EPILOGUE]

I'm sitting at the kitchen table reading, and my wife, Beth, is at the sink washing dishes. It's been two years since I got out of jail. I set the book down and look up at her. She's small, and she has blond hair, and although I can't see them at the moment, her eyes are green. I imagine that I can make out a faint smile on her lips. I imagine that she's smiling because she's content, because this is a safe and comfortable home that we have together. She smiles because she's happy, and she loves me.

I light a cigarette, and sort of marvel at what an amazingly good place and time this is. I feel a warm balloon in my chest, and I want to break apart because happiness, true happiness, is an unusual and suspicious thing. Right on the heels of this feeling comes the thought that it could end at any moment. Anything could happen.

It's hot and the kitchen door is open. Beth can be seen from the alley that runs behind our house and I can hear a couple kids walking down the alley, making a lot of noise.

I hear one of them say, "Hey, look at that."

The other one says, "Aw, man. Sweet piece of fucking ass."

"You can do my dishes, baby!"

"And suck my dick!"

I sigh, shake my head, and get my shoes on. I go outside. I watch the kids go into a video store a block away, and I follow them in. They're younger than I'd expected, thirteen, fourteen years old. I go up to them and say, "Hey."

They turn around. I probably look like I'm about to smash their faces in, because they're scared shitless.

"You guys yell at that girl back there?"

"No," one of them says. "We didn't do anything."

The other one says, "We were just playing around."

"Well, watch what you say. Somebody's likely to beat your fucking asses."

I turn around and walk out.

I've scared the kids, but this doesn't mean they've necessarily learned anything. In fact, I assume it makes things worse. Their fear probably turns immediately to indignation. Who's that fucker think he is? I have to wonder if they will eventually ambush me with baseball bats in the alley. Some kids are capable of anything.

I go back into the apartment and kiss Beth on the cheek.

"You didn't beat them up or anything, did you?" she asks.

"No," I say. "I didn't. They're just kids."

ACKNOWLEDGMENTS

I want to thank my agent, Dan Lazar (not just for his editorial insight but for his astonishing ability to make me feel like I am his only client, by his constant availability, his concern, and his dedication to his work and to mine, even though I've badgered the hell out of him and probably driven him crazy). Dan, I am amazed by your professionalism.

I want to thank my editor, Margaret Miller, for her wonderful insight, for helping craft this work into a polished piece of damn-near-perfect beauty. I will always be grateful. Thank you for making this book a reality, for having the guts and the awareness to know what it means.

And thank you, Jenavieve, my wife, for loving me and suffering with me and for me, and for your patience and your sanity, all of which have saved me more than once during this whole process. And, Ross Rosenberg, thank you for all your help and encouragement. And,

ACKNOWLEDGMENTS

Dan O'Reilly, thank you as well, for everything. And of course . . . thank you, Mom, for encouraging me during all of this, even though most of the stuff in this book came as a complete surprise to you.

And thank you, Gavin Rose of the ACLU of Indiana, for fighting the good fight and winning, and giving me hope when there was none.